LEAVE YOUR WATER JAR

WATER JAR

Breaking the Bondage of Past Sins

Georgia Wilkerson

Foreword by James Hutchings

www.xulonpress.com

DEDICATION

To my three children, Margaret Angeline, Nathan Terry, and Robbie Anita, who have allowed me the privilege of being honest, open, and upfront about my past hurts, sins, and failures, as well as any minute accomplishments I have experienced along my journey, thereby encouraging and aiding in my deliverance from years of bondage—who have loved me in spite of my shortcomings, and for whom I pray they will break the chain of generational sins (whatever those sins may be) for their children and their children's children, each one learning to *leave his/ her water jar,* and for whom I hope to leave a legacy of a Godly lifestyle and the freedom that comes in truly trusting Christ in and for everything, I lovingly and passionately dedicate this book.

ACKNOWLEDGEMENTS

Obviously, more than just the words from the author's pen are involved in the writing of any book. I want to say a special "thank you" to the people that gave of themselves in order that this book would become a reality.

- Karen Gilbert, my sister and the youngest of us five kids, took the time to answer my many questions. She is a Christian counselor whose experience and wisdom provided what was needed to bridge the gap between the relational issues of believers today and the relational issues of the woman at the well.
- Linda Patterson, my sister and the oldest of us five kids, took time from her hectic schedule to proofread the manuscript. Her experience as an educator, at the college level and now for Sylvan Learning Centers, provided the

constructive criticism necessary to ensure the book's readability and grammatical accuracy.

• Each of my three children listened as I explained what I was feeling and how I identified with the woman at well in many ways. They read the manuscript and offered encouragement for me to be more specific in certain areas and more discreet in other areas.

Words cannot express my gratitude. Your contributions to this work are immeasurable.

CONTENTS

Chapter

Dedication v
Acknowledgements vii
Foreword xi
Introduction xiii

1. Divine Appointment 19
2. Desensitized 35
3. Demoralized 53
4. Destitute 81
5. Destroyed 113
6. Delivered 139
7. Directive for Freedom 157

FOREWORD

There is a battle raging between God and Satan
for the mind of every Christian. Even after
salvation, we are vulnerable to the temptation to let
our past dominate how we view ourselves today.
Although the soul of a Christian is saved once and
for all when he/she publicly confesses his/her sin,
there continues to be a war between the temptations
of the mind and the spirit-filled life. Why is this so?
Could it be because we continue to hold on to our
"water jars"?

This book, based on the account of "the woman
at the well" found in John's Gospel chapter four, is a
refreshing look at what it means to leave your "water
jar" and move forward for the glory of our Lord with
new joy, peace, and a love for life in our newfound
relationship in Christ. Author Georgia Wilkerson
gives fresh, new insight into this age-old account
that can be the catalyst to set the reader free from
the power of Satan that holds him/her in bondage to

a past that is under the blood of Christ—forgiven, never to be remembered by the loving Father God against him/her ever again. It is amazing how the truth in this book can set one free to enjoy their new life in Christ to the fullest.

This book is about hope and the provisions our loving Heavenly Father has made for us to enjoy the love, joy, and peace discussed in the Scriptures. There is hope for you to change your life of unhappiness and struggle. You have been saved! God wants you to be a happy child of His! Why not leave your old "water jar" and begin to live as a child of the King should live?

Now, thank God, this gifted author, Georgia Wilkerson, has gone right into the heart of John chapter four with a pungent, powerful, but practical insight. Anyone reading this book will be blessed, instructed, warmed, and challenged. My sincere prayer is that the truth taught in this volume will be a blessing to thousands of Christian men and women who struggle to break free from their self-imposed guilt over past, but forgiven, sin because they keep returning to their old useless "water jars."

Dr. James C. Hutchings, D.Min.
Registrar, Covington Theological Seminary
Ft. Oglethorpe, GA

INTRODUCTION

"18For I know that nothing good lives in me, that is, in my flesh. For the desire to do what is good is with me, but there is no ability to do it. ¹⁹For I do not do the good that I want to do, but I practice the evil that I do not want to do. ²⁰Now if I do what I do not want, I am no longer the one doing it, but it is the sin that lives in me. ²¹So I discover this principle: when I want to do good, evil is with me. ²²For in my inner self I joyfully agree with God's law. ²³But I see a different law in the parts of my body, waging war against the law of my mind and taking me prisoner to the law of sin in the parts of my body. ²⁴What a wretched man I am! Who will rescue me from this body of death? ²⁵I thank God through Jesus Christ our Lord! So then, with my mind I myself am a slave to the law of God, but with my flesh, to the law of sin" (Romans 7:18-25, HCSB).

After having placed my trust in Christ as a seven-year-old girl, I spent many years with the same struggle the Apostle Paul expressed in Romans chapter seven, verses eighteen through twenty-five. In reality, I stopped short of verse twenty-five, and for some reason, I did not quite grasp the significance of this verse—"I thank God through Jesus Christ our Lord!" I failed to understand that the Holy Spirit, through Paul, was telling me this: *I cannot be good—I'm thankful it is done through the grace of Jesus Christ who will deliver me!* Thus, my struggles continued, not only continued, but also worsened.

However, because the struggles continued, I began to question "why?" *Why do I, as well as many other born-again believers in Christ, have such difficulty living in surrender and obedience to Christ? I do not want to sin; I do not want to make the wrong choices, so why do I continue in such destructive behaviors? If we are really the relational creatures that Christian pastors, teachers, and psychologists/ counselors assert we are, then why do so many of us experience such difficulty with relationships?*

In 2001 I was intensely writing a thirteen-week Ladies' Bible Study on the Book of John that I was to teach at our church titled, *Absolute Deity—A Look At The Book of John From A Woman's Perspective.* The writing of the lessons from John chapters one through three had gone extremely well and my passion for the Word was growing. As I was writing the lesson on John chapter four, the woman at the well, it seemed that all insight the Lord had given me became stagnated, but I continued to pray for the Holy Spirit's guidance—for Him to teach me the Word.

"What is it about her life that I am unable to comprehend?" I kept asking myself. I felt that there was something more than what appeared on the surface. It was not long before God revealed that my insight had not become stagnant, but, instead, He was inviting me to delve deeper into His Word and in relationship with Him. Then verse twenty-eight seemed to literally jump off the page and into my heart. Oh, the many times I had read this verse without understanding! "Then the woman **left** her water jar" (John 4:28a; emphasis mine).

On this particular day, I not only understood that she left her water jar at the feet of Jesus in exchange for Living Water, but I also, for the first time, became conscious of the fact that it is not recorded she ever went back to the well and picked it up again. It then became obvious to me her water jar represented more than just a vessel for drawing water from the well. Instead, the water jar represents all of her futile attempts to find love, peace, and significance through her many relationships, etcetera, and so it goes for us. It was then I understood the reason for many of my struggles and failures as I continually used the things in my water jar to satisfy needs in my life only Jesus could satisfy.

Because of the fact that we live in a sin-cursed world and we are sinners by nature as well as sinners by choice, we constantly struggle with trying to meet our needs in our way rather than trusting God to meet **every** need in life, in the way He knows is best. It is not that we give back or reject the gift of salvation we have accepted each time we return and pick up our water jar, but rather we somehow feel God saved us and then left us to carry on the best we can. We allow what appears logical and reasonable to override our faith. Therefore, out of fear of the unknown, we turn to the familiar things of our water jars to bring hope, joy, love, and significance to our lives. However, rather than setting us free from painful past experiences, our water jars will only enslave us.

At first glance, this book may appear to be my personal testimony; in reading further, you may think the purpose of this book is to offer emotional and spiritual counsel; then you may decide this book is nothing more than an easy-reading novel. In truth, *Leave Your Water Jar* is all of these. This book contains my personal testimony, including my testimony of salvation and the times I went back to the well and picked up my water jar after placing my faith and trust in Christ. In addition, I believe this book will offer Godly, sound advice and counsel that will encourage the reader to leave his/her water jar, breaking free from the bondage of past sins and destructive behaviors.

Finally, beginning in chapter three the reader will find a mini-novel, which continues through chapter six of the book. I decided that through a mini-novel the possible reasons for this woman's demise could be better communicated. The woman at the well, whom I have compassionately named Prisoner in the novel, represents all of us.

While parts of the mini-novel are my true story, I do not want the reader to focus on me and the difficulties I experienced, because other portions could possibly be your story as well. Rather, it is my intention to help us all reach a better understanding of the woman at the well, the struggles she encountered, and the deliverance she finally found in Christ. I desire for each reader of this book to find freedom in Christ, which only comes when we are willing to leave our water jars at the feet of Jesus and never pick them up again.

CHAPTER ONE

Divine Appointment

Day in and day out, much of our time is spent frantically rushing here and rushing there trying to make sure we are not late for that important appointment. We have to meet with this client, make that phone call, catch the plane, close this deal, and... Of course, in our spare time we drive the kids to school, pick the kids up from school, drive them to music lessons, or to ball practice, or dance lessons, and/or all of the above and much more.

Life is hectic! Many times, life is not just hectic, but also is cluttered with the wrong things. Okay, maybe it is not cluttered with the *wrong* things, just *unnecessary* things.

In your mind's eye, try to visualize what a snapshot of your life on a typical day would look like. No doubt, it would resemble the disarray of the average teenager's room. You would find clothes strewn on the floor as you questioned, which is the dirty pile and which is the clean pile? "I must find exactly the right thing to wear. I have an appointment today with the *big* boss." You throw clothes right and left before finally deciding on just the right outfit. "Oh no, I've got to scoot; I can't be late—not today of all days!" Please, do not overlook the plate of three-fourths eaten pizza and the half-empty soda can on the nightstand. You barely make it to that important luncheon, sliding onto your chair in the nick of time like a *big-league slugger* sliding in at home plate. Then there was not enough time to finish lunch before dashing off to the next appointment.

There are many appointments throughout life—some, necessary—some, unnecessary—some, **divine**. Have you ever experienced a divine appointment—you know, those appointments God arranges that are set by the Heavenly Schedule-Setter? You were at the right place at the right time, and you were able to share the good news of Christ with someone. Or perhaps your being at the right place at the right time enabled you to share an encouraging word with a brother or sister. Maybe you were, instead, the recipient of the encouragement. It could even be that you were detained somewhere, thereby narrowly escaping some potential danger. I am talking about those times when you knew the events of the day could not be mere coincidence. Now, in retrospect, you have come to realize that those events were a *God-thing*—a divine appointment.

It is an awesome, yet humbling, experience to know there was a divine appointment on your spiritual daily planner and you kept the appointment, thus fulfilling God's plan and purpose for that particular time in your life. One major concern I have for myself is that I would possibly be late for that appointment or, perhaps even worse, I would be unable to recognize a divine appointment in the midst of all of life's clutter.

The most exciting piece of historical literature I have ever read, the Bible, is packed full with one divine appointment after another. It is truly adventuresome reading when you begin to notice in the Scriptures how divine appointments were scheduled, how circumstances were employed of Almighty God to carry out those appointments, and how the cast of characters in the narratives reacted to those divine appointments.

Moses had a divine appointment with a bush, which was on fire, yet was not consumed. Moses was faced with the choice of whether or not he would keep such an appointment. The Bible tells us in Exodus chapter three, verse three that when Moses saw the bush on fire, he said he would go and check this thing out: "Then Moses said, 'I will now turn aside and see this great sight, why the bush does not burn'." (NKJV) Verse four of chapter three yields further evidence that this was truly a divine appointment: "So when the LORD saw that he turned aside to look, God called to him from the midst of the bush and said, 'Moses, Moses'!" (Exodus 3:4a&b, NKJV)

In the story of the two spies whom Joshua sent to view the land, especially Jericho, we find a twofold divine appointment. The two spies went to their divine appointment with Rahab, the harlot, by which they found refuge from danger, escaping destruction at the hands of the king of Jericho. Because Rahab kept her divine appointment in providing safety for these two men, she found mercy and grace. When the city was utterly destroyed, Rahab, although an inhabitant of Jericho with a house located in the city's wall, was saved. In fact, she is in the ancestral line of the Messiah, Jesus Christ (Matthew 1:5-6).

Since we are speaking of divine appointments, it is certainly appropriate to make mention of Ruth, the Moabite widowed daughter-in-law of Naomi. Naomi, her husband, and their two sons were originally from Bethlehem, but had moved to Moab because of a famine that plagued Judah. In the course of time, Naomi's husband died, and each of her two sons chose to marry Moabite women. After the death of her two sons, Naomi decided to go home to Bethlehem. As you recall, Ruth insisted on staying with her mother-in-law and moved back to Bethlehem with her.

Personally, I feel this story reflects a string of many divine appointments, but the one that really stands out in my mind was scheduled after Ruth had come to Bethlehem. Ruth had a divine appointment at a threshing floor where she found her *Kinsman Redeemer*, Boaz. She is also listed in the genealogy of Christ (Matthew 1:5-6).

It would be an injustice to overlook the miraculous birth of Samuel. Hannah, his mother, had been unable to conceive. If this was not bad enough, her husband's other wife, Peninnah, who had children, would scoff Hannah cruelly because of her barrenness. Hannah, however, was faithful to keep the divine appointment at the Lord's house every year. She prayed and wept many tears, and "the LORD remembered her" (1Samuel 1:19c, HCSB). Hannah gave birth to a son, Samuel, and she kept the vow she had made, giving Samuel to the Lord once he was weaned.

It is so exciting to read in the Scriptures about the many divine appointments of Jesus, the Son of God. When Jesus walked the earth, shrouded in human flesh, the places He went and the people He met were not the result of sheer chance. Everything Jesus did, everywhere Jesus went, and everyone Jesus met had been foreordained according to God's foreknowledge and was in accordance with the *heavenly timetable*.

It was not happenstance that Jesus and His disciples attended a marriage in Cana where He turned water into wine, thus manifesting His glory (John 2). Another time when Jesus was in Cana of Galilee, a nobleman begged Jesus to heal his son who was at the point of death. This incident was not a matter of luck or good fortune, but rather a divine appointment. Jesus did not merely *happen* to go again to Cana, and the nobleman did not just *happen* to hear that Jesus had come from Judea to Galilee (John 4). No! Indeed, this was a divine appointment and "Jesus said to him, 'Go your way; your son lives.' So the man believed the word Jesus spoke to him, and he went his way" (John 4:50, NKJV).

Let us not overlook the healing at the pool of Bethesda in Jerusalem. This pool was located by the Sheep Gate, no less. Do you honestly think for one minute that it just happened that the Lamb of God entered through the Sheep Gate? Can you simply chalk up to fate the fact that out of all the sick people lying around the pool, Jesus went to only this one man—and on a Sabbath, yet (John 5:1-16)? I don't think so! This can only be viewed as a divine appointment.

During His earthly ministry, sometimes the people in need came to Jesus, and sometimes He went to the people. The book of John is sated with the relating of divine appointments on Jesus' *heavenly schedule* during His mission on earth. One of my favorites, and one from which I have learned a great deal, is Jesus' divine appointment with the Samaritan woman at Jacob's well (John 4).

In John chapter four, we find Jesus going *out of His way*, so to speak, to a woman of ill repute—a sinner. I say that Jesus went *out of His way* because, for the most part, Jews ordinarily avoided any and all associations with the Samaritans. So high and wide was the wall of prejudice and so great was their hatred toward each other that when traveling from Judea to Galilee, and vice versa, the Jews would take a longer route in order to avoid going through Samaria.

This great animosity was the result of the Assyrian invasion of the northern kingdom of Israel in 727 BC. The Israelites who were not deported, but had remained in their homeland, intermarried with the Assyrians who had taken over the rule in Israel. The Samaritans were half-breeds and could not prove their genealogy—that they were children of Israel. Therefore, the ethnic tension and hatred grew, as did the chasm between the Jews and Samaritans. The hatred was so great they refused to worship together, and the Samaritans set up their own place of worship on Mt. Gerizim. In fact, some Pharisees prayed that no Samaritan would be raised in the resurrection — further proof of their hatred for each other.

The Samaritans were considered to be a most undesirable element of society. They were rejected by almost everyone around them because they were not totally of Jewish descent. At the same time, they were not totally of Assyrian descent. They were social outcasts. However, the woman at Jacob's well was not just an outcast in the same sense as other Samaritans — she was *really* an outcast.

This woman was socially outcast because of her race, as is understood by the preceding paragraphs, but she was also an outcast because of her gender. Most men of this time had very little esteem for women. Women were viewed as second-class citizens. The custom was that a woman was not to be saluted or spoken to in public. In other words, a man should not say "hello" to a woman he met on the street; he shouldn't even tip his turban as a gesture of greeting. Perhaps now you understand why his disciples were so amazed that Jesus was talking with a woman (John 4:27).

Thirdly, this woman was outcast because of her lifestyle. She was shunned, mocked, and ridiculed by the other women in town. No doubt, there was a lot of whispering going on at the well when the women came to perform their expected chore of drawing water twice each day (Genesis 24:11). It is also obvious this woman had relational issues; she had been married five times and was, at this time, living with a man who was not her husband. In light of the custom of the day concerning women and the life-style that held this woman captive, it becomes clear as to the reason this woman was not surprised that a man spoke to her in public. She was only surprised by the fact that a Jew spoke to her in public (John 4:9).

In the opening verses of John chapter four, we see the Pharisees inciting competition between Jesus and John the Baptist with the result being Jesus decided to leave Judea and go to Galilee. Remember, the shorter route from Judea to Galilee was through Samaria, but the Jews usually opted for the longer route in order to avoid all associations with the Samaritans. However, on this particular occasion Jesus needed to go through Samaria because He had a divine appointment with a woman, a *social outcast*, who was in dire need of *living water* and He could not, would not, be late.

I love the way the King James Version translates this passage, in particular, verses three and four: "He left Judea, and departed again into Galilee. And he **must needs** go through Samaria" (John 4:3-4, KJV; emphasis mine). Why don't we take a look at the meaning of these two words—must and needs? Perhaps this will give some insight as to why I find the wording of the King James Version in verse four so fascinating. Take note of the meanings from the *Webster's New Dictionary of the English Language*:

- ¹**must** *vb*—used as an auxiliary especially to express a command, requirement, obligation, or necessity
- ²**must** *n* **1:** an imperative duty **2:** an indispensable item
- **needs** *adv*: of necessity: NECESSARILY (must **needs** be recognized)

Could we say Jesus felt an obligation to go through Samaria? And would we be correct in saying that Jesus indispensably needed to take this particular route from Judea to Galilee? Could it be said Jesus realized He had an obligation of an absolutely essential nature, which required Him to go through Samaria rather than around Samaria? YES! YES! YES! Hallelujah, Jesus did not just *want* to go through Samaria; He *needed* to go through Samaria. I feel it safe to say Jesus felt a compelling obligation to take this particular route because He had a divine appointment with a woman who was desperate for a *drink* of water.

I suppose it is for these reasons this particular divine appointment in Scripture is so precious to me. There was a time Jesus went *out of His way* to keep a divine appointment with a seven-year-old girl. I am sure there are some who would say that a girl of seven could not be a sinner and would not be in need of salvation at such a young age. However, we are all sinners in need of a Savior; it does not matter if a person is seven or ninety-seven. When Jesus comes to keep a divine appointment with someone, it is of utmost, eternal importance that the person does not miss this divine appointment. Praise God, I am so thankful Jesus loved me enough to come to me in my hour of need.

In all honesty, I have missed some divine appointments in my life—some because I was too busy and some because I simply did not discern correctly. However, I am sure of this one fact: as a seven-year-old child, I did not miss, nor was I late for, my divine appointment when I met the Savior and placed my trust in Him.

My family and I lived six miles outside the small town of Watertown, Tennessee. My mother had grown up in the Cumberland Presbyterian Church, and my father had grown up in the Catholic Church, or at least he attended a Catholic school through the eighth grade in Kenosha, Wisconsin. Rather than drive six miles to town every Sunday to attend the Cumberland Presbyterian Church, we attended a little Baptist Church, Ramah Baptist Church, which was only about a mile from our house. My mother and father both joined this church, and they made sure the entire family was in church every time the church doors were open—without exception.

For as long as I can remember, I have extremely enjoyed going to church. I loved the singing! I loved my Sunday school class! I loved Vacation Bible School! I must confess, however, that to a little girl of five years of age, sometimes it seemed as though the preacher would never stop preaching. This was especially true of those long, hot, summer nights during Revival Meetings. In a little country church with no air-conditioning, I sat for what seemed like hours frantically fanning myself to stay cool. The windows were open wide as moths and mosquitoes poured in by the droves.

Usually, our pianist and music director would step aside during these meetings for someone of more talent. To this music-lover, that was a real treat. It was not that our own pianist and music director could not do the job; it was just nice to hear someone different and hear some new songs. I always made it fine through the time of music, but the mono-toned preaching along with the hot, humid air would cause me to fall asleep every time. Before long, my fan with the picture of *The Last Supper* on it would begin to slow its forward and backward motion, my head would rest against the back of the pew, my eyelids would begin to feel like they weighed a ton, until finally, I would curl up on the pew and get, what seemed to be at that time, the best sleep I ever had in my life.

At some point along the way, though I cannot determine exactly when, the preaching did not seem quite as monotonous as it had before. Perhaps the pastor was practicing his sermons, or maybe he was spending more time in study and preparation. I am not really sure what made the difference, but shortly after my sixth birthday, I began to listen more intently to the Word—both in Sunday school and in the preaching. No longer did I fall asleep in church as easily as before, even on those hot summer nights.

Called Out

As I listened and comprehended more of the Scriptures, there were times when I felt as though the pastor was preaching to no one except me. Oh sure, I was aware of all the people sitting around me, but it seemed that the pastor's long, skinny finger was always pointed at me when he said, "I know there is someone here today who needs to be saved—someone needs to give their heart to Jesus." In this respect, I can relate to the woman at Jacob's well.

Jesus arrived at the well at approximately six in the evening. Since it was customary for the women to come to the well and draw water at six in the morning and again at six in the evening (Genesis 24:11), we can assume this woman was not the only one at the well, yet she is the only one to whom Jesus spoke. Jesus called her out of the crowd, and as I received more and more of God's light, I felt as though I was being called out of the crowd—like the sermon was for no one but me.

Convicted

When Jesus comes back, what will it be like? What happens to us when we die? Why did Jesus have to die on the cross? How can a person know if he/she will go to heaven when they die? How can a person know if he/she will go to heaven when they die? My questioning went on and on nonstop! There was so much I did not understand, but I wanted to know more.

By the time my seventh birthday rolled around, I began to feel, not just inquisitive, but rather uneasy about the fact that "we have all sinned and come short of the glory of God" (Romans 3:23, KJV). Somewhere along the line, the words of Romans 3:23 became very personal, and I was convicted of my sin. No longer was it simply a matter that *everyone* has sinned, but it was a conviction that *I* had sinned and needed Jesus to be my own, personal Savior. Just like the woman at the well (John 4:16-18), I had been confronted with the reality of my sin, and the Holy Spirit convicted me of my need.

Even though as a seven-year-old girl I did not know how to formulate my thoughts and express my feelings, I knew I needed Jesus and that without Him my destiny was hell. There was a constant churning in my soul, especially when I heard sermons about the Second Coming of Christ; I was so afraid Jesus would come back and I would be left behind.

Now, since I was only seven years of age, it must be understood that there was no conviction about the many wrong things I had done, for I had not lived long enough to have committed anything that in the opinion of most people would be considered sin. Nonetheless, I understood God is holy, and the fact that I had heard the Word, done something that was seemingly so small as telling a little *white* lie, and had not yet accepted God's great salvation, qualified me as a sinner and disqualified me from heaven.

Converted

Evidently, it was more than obvious to every one that I was struggling. My Sunday school teacher would give me a look as if to say, "I'm praying for you; I sense your conviction." My father often questioned me about how much I understood concerning my need to be saved. A few times on the way home from church, he would make statements like, "I thought sure you would be saved today." Before you begin thinking, *Wow, her father was terribly pushy,* let me just say, it was all because of his concern for me. I need to add that I did not want to receive Christ in order to please my father or my mother. Contrariwise, I understood I was a sinner and that I needed—wanted—Jesus. I wanted to know I would go to heaven when I died.

In the summer of 1961, another Revival Meeting rolled around. Most likely, it was the last week of July because our church always had its Revival Meeting the last week of July. I especially looked forward to this meeting; somehow, I just felt like this was *my* time—that I would receive Christ before the week was over.

My father was out of town with his work, but mother made sure we were in church every service that week. On Tuesday night, instead of sitting with my best friend as I normally did, I sat with my oldest sister on the second pew from the front. As the preacher preached, I felt as though my heart would jump out of my chest. I could not wait for the preacher to finish his sermon so I could go to the altar and be saved. At some point, I wrote a note to my big sister that read, "Tonight I am going to become a *C*." Then I leaned over and whispered to her, "That stands for Christian; I didn't know how to spell it."

Finally, the preacher finished, and the invitation hymn began. I do not recall what the sermon was about, but the hymn, "Oh Why Not Tonight" still plays vividly in my head:

Oh, do not let the Word depart,
And close thine eyes against the light;
Poor sinner, harden not your heart,
Be saved, oh, tonight.
(Words by Elizabeth Reed; Music by J. Calvin Bushy)

As this song was being sung, I stepped into the aisle and went to the altar where my pastor met me and asked, "Why have you come tonight?" I replied, "I want to be saved." I had trusted Christ to forgive my sin and save me the moment I took that first step toward Him. This was my point of conversion, for like the Samaritan woman (John 4:28-30), I left my water jar at the feet of Jesus, received a drink of *living water*, and then confessed publicly that Jesus is **my** Savior and Lord. My water jar, which represented all of my *good-little-girl things* I had used in attempts to satisfy the God-thirst within me, I left at Jesus' feet in exchange for peace and satisfaction that can only be found in the water He gives.

Oh yes, divine appointments! Over the years, I have encountered many divine appointments, but none will ever overshadow the divine appointment of that Tuesday night in July 1961, when Jesus became my very own. I had always loved Him—ever since I had first heard about Him in Sunday school. However, now I didn't just know *about* Him. I had experienced a divine appointment, and now I *know* Him—personally.

Jesus, I thank You for divine appointments—especially the divine appointment when You extended to me Your great salvation!

If you have never left your water jar at Jesus' feet in exchange for a drink of Living Water, I would like to invite you to do so at this time. It is as simple as A-B-C. ***Admit*** you are a sinner, because "all have sinned and fall short of the glory of God" (Romans 3:23). "***Believe*** in your heart that God has raised Him from the dead, you will be saved" (Romans 10:9b). ***Confess*** or **call** on Jesus because "if you **confess** with your mouth the Lord Jesus and believe in your heart that God has raised Him from the dead, you will be saved" (Romans 10:9). "Whoever **calls** on the name of the LORD shall be saved" (Romans 10:13).

A divine appointment has been arranged *just for you*! Jesus is tenderly waiting and wooing you to Himself, and this is one divine appointment you do not want to miss. Please, do not be late!

CHAPTER TWO

Desensitized

It is so amazing that when a person is young, young in the Lord, their heart is tender and they are so sensitive to the Holy Spirit—to what is right and wrong. I remember the feelings of being a new Christian. I was so sensitive, not only to God's constant presence in my life, but also to actions that were pleasing to Him and actions that were not pleasing to Him.

Even as a seven-year-old, I was eager to learn more of Jesus. Every Sunday I was glad to report to my Sunday school teacher that I had read my Bible everyday the week before. However, I was not comprehending very much of what I read, and it was not long before this everyday Bible reading became nothing more than a ritual and drudgery, which soon dwindled to nada. It would have been so nice if, way back when I was a kid, there had been some translations of the Bible that were more readable and understandable for a seven-year-old than the King James Version. No, I am not knocking the King James Version. As a matter of fact, I am very thankful King James and his scholars provided a copy of the Bible to the English-speaking people. You must admit, however, it is not easy reading and/or comprehension for a child born in the twentieth century.

During my childhood, I had some good, godly teachers and pastors, but discipleship was minuscule in that little country church. Think about this for a moment: You take a child who is eager to learn, but does not have a copy of the Scripture that is written in an easily understood manner and Sunday school teachers and preachers who fail to bridge the gap between the *back then—way back when* and the *here and now* and you have a runt of a Christian.

We are commanded to grow, spiritually. First Peter chapter two, verse two tells us to desire the pure, unadulterated milk of the word for the purpose of growing. When I was first saved, I wanted to grow in my walk with the Lord. I truly desired the sincere milk of the word. I did not want to be spiritually anemic and have my growth severely stunted. However, I needed help in receiving spiritual food, and it appeared there was no help for me.

You see, *to grow or not to grow, that is the question*, and each individual believer in Christ must answer that question for himself/herself. While it would have been nice to have had some help with my spiritual growth, the time quickly came for me to take responsibility in this area of my life. Unfortunately, I did not assume this responsibility until I was much older and had experienced a lot of heartache. Instead, I blamed others for my spiritual inadequacy and lack of growth. Oh sure, more mature Christians should mentor babies in Christ and be actively involved in their discipleship, but ultimately each believer is responsible for whether or not they are going to grow up.

Failure to get into the Scriptures, learn of Christ, and grow in grace and knowledge are only the beginning elements to building a wall that will block your fellowship with the Heavenly Father. If you have truly been saved, then you belong to Christ forever (John 3:16 & 10:28-29), but when you are not growing in your walk with the Lord you become less and less sensitive to the voice of the Holy Spirit as brick upon brick is laid in this wall of broken fellowship.

Let me remind you that the Enemy is very clever, but at the same time, he really has no new tricks. One of his primary strategies against newborn babes in the faith is to desensitize them concerning right and wrong. The dictionary definition of *desensitize* is, "to make insensitive or nonreactive to a sensitizing agent." For the born-again believer, the sensitizing agent is the Holy Spirit who lives inside him/her. He causes us to be sensitive to what is right and what is wrong. Since the Holy Spirit teaches us God's word and brings to our remembrance what Jesus said (John 14:26), we must be internalizing the Scriptures in order for Him to have the means whereby He makes us sensitive. If you are not growing in your faith, then most likely this process of desensitization is already beginning to take place.

The desensitization is usually a very subtle and gradual process. It begins with our not taking in enough of the Word. Then we start to allow things to enter the gateways to our minds—things such as TV shows, music, movies, books, magazines, internet images, and filthy talk that we know cannot edify us in any way whatsoever! Unlike the computer, which I used to type this manuscript, the material embedded in the computer of your mind cannot be deleted. You can constantly fill your mind with so much of Jesus that you hardly ever think of those things anymore, but those images and words are stored in the memory banks of your mind for as long as you live on this earth, and when you let down your guard, the Enemy will use those things to condemn and accuse you.

The Church of the Living God is sick, very sick indeed. Overall, we have lost our ability to distinguish between right and wrong because we have become so worldly-minded. We have become desensitized!

For example, on the average television sitcom, they take God's name in vain with every other breath and we (Christians) think nothing of it. I am not simply referring to the use of euphemisms, but rather to the use of the holy name of God in an irreverent manner. Nevertheless, we continue to sit in front of this one-eyed monster and allow these words to fill our minds. One thing that is so sad is many people who profess to know Christ use this same kind of language every day and see nothing wrong in doing so!

God's name should never be used as part of an exclamatory phrase expressing surprise, unbelief, disgust, and etcetera. Do you understand what I am saying? Do I need to spell it out for you? We have grown too accustomed to hearing cursing and the taking of God's name in vain because we have become insensitive to the sensitizing agent in our lives—the Holy Spirit.

If the language is not bad enough, then we must deal with the violence in many TV programs, music, and movies. It really got under my skin a few years ago to hear Christian parents talk about how they thought Mel Gibson's movie, *The Passion of the Christ*, was much too violent. However, these same parents and their kids ignored the violence of television and movies, as they sat watching someone bash another persons head against a concrete floor until their brains oozed from the cranium. Oh, let us not forget the many sexual innuendos, although, many more times than not, the sexual content is much more than insinuation. When the program is rated with the letters D, L, S, SC, and/or V, which stands for dress (immodest), language (profanity and/or obscenity), sex, sexual content, and violence that should let you know it is not material with which you want to fill your mind.

Clay Crosse, the well-known contemporary Christian artist, is very open and honest about his addiction to pornography. He almost lost his family, but sought help and was able to overcome his addiction. Clay shares that he knows he was saved at age thirteen but, like so many of us, did not grow a lot in his walk with the Lord. His first exposure to pornographic material was at the house of a friend whose father had a porn magazine. I do not know if his friend or his friend's father professed to know Christ, but there are many professing Christians who have trouble knowing whether something is pornographic.

Clay shares that his pornography addiction began some years before, but he thought that once he got married he would not have any more problems in this area. For a while after his marriage, this lustful appetite was suppressed, but then it reared its ugly head when he and his wife started watching television programs they knew contained material a Christian should not be watching. He was slowly, but surely, becoming desensitized to the voice of the Holy Spirit.

"Oh, I can handle it! All of this garbage I put into my mind does not affect me in any way whatsoever." Then, why do you feel as though you must see that next episode or listen to the lyrics of that song or go to that website? Let's just assume for a moment that you *can* handle it—even though if you are honest with yourself you know you cannot—but let's assume these things will not affect you, then stop and ask yourself some questions: *If it is not wrong for me to view these TV programs, movies, websites, and listen to profanity or seductive and/or violent song lyrics, is it what is best? Are these things going to build up my faith, or do they have the potential to tear down my faith? Will this hurt my testimony and/or cause a brother or sister in Christ to stumble? Will this hurt my testimony and hinder someone from being saved? If it is not wrong, is it expedient for me?*

The Apostle Paul said, "All things are lawful for me, but all things are not expedient: all things are lawful for me, but all things edify not" (1Corinthians 10:23, KJV). In other words, if it is not to the advantage of your spiritual growth, if it is not profitable for you, if you will not be better because of these actions, and if you are not sure it is going to be good for you and those you influence then do not deliberately put these things in your mind.

Desensitized! I remember the first time that I heard a curse word on TV. That word came from the mouth of Johnny Carson on the *Tonight Show*. My parents were also sitting in the room watching this program with me. As I sat there wide-eyed staring at the screen, I thought—*Did my parents hear that? Surely they did. Well, they didn't say anything about it, so I guess it is okay if someone on TV says that—just as long as that word never comes out of my mouth.*

Thus, my desensitization began. Do you know what? It was not long before that particular word and many more curse words began to flow from my mouth. I felt bad when a curse word would slip through my lips, but at the same time, I would justify my speech with excuses such as: *You have to say something when you are mad, etcetera. Everybody talks like that. As long as I don't take God's name in vain, there is really nothing wrong with it.* Can you understand that my insensitivity to God's voice was escalating, as was my downward spiral into a host of wrong choices?

Desensitization, for me, began when I allowed filthy talk to enter my ears, and I continued to become desensitized when I started viewing ungodly images with my eyes. To avoid the downfall caused by becoming desensitized, David, through inspiration of the Holy Spirit, made this vow of integrity: "I will live with integrity of heart in my house. I will not set anything godless before my eyes. I hate the doing of transgression; it will not cling to me" (Psalm 101:2c-3, HCSB). Perhaps we need to keep this Scripture plastered to our TV and computer screens or on our wallets so it is visible when we are ready to enter a cinema, buy a magazine, or rent a movie.

The Apostle Paul gives further instruction concerning the language we use and/or deliberately put into our ears: "But now you must also **put away** all of the following: ... and **filthy language** from your mouth" (Colossians 3:8, HCSB; emphasis mine). In the book of Ephesians we are instructed that "No rotten talk should come from your mouth, but only what is good for the building up of someone in need, in order to give grace to those who hear" (Ephesians 4:29, HCSB).

When we allow Satan the opportunity to desensitize us—make us insensitive or nonreactive to the Holy Spirit's guidance—we will make poor choices, and sometimes, destructive choices, which we vowed we would never make. This desensitization process skews our thinking. We come to the point where we are unable to think straight, so we make wrong choices. We constantly feed the flesh instead of feeding the spirit because our thinking is distorted, and, if left unchecked, wrong thinking results in wrong actions.

I heard on the news that the executives of the at-present popular TV series, *24*, were planning to tone down some of the violence that is so graphic in this show. Because the show depicts terrorist activity against the United States, they had received a lot of criticism from our military. However, the criticism from the military was not the primary reason for their decision. Their decision was based on the fact that their viewing audience had become numb to the violence — it did not thrill them as it once did.

America, in general, has become desensitized, not only to right and wrong, but also simply to things decent and indecent and to things sacred and profane. For many years, it has been the agenda of Hollywood, the music industry, and our public school system, just to name a few entities, to desensitize us. Do you remember how Satan deceived Eve in the Garden of Eden? He sowed the seed of doubt by asking one simple question: "Yea, hath God said, 'Ye shall not eat of every tree of the garden' " (Genesis 3:2, KJV)?

Thus, it has been down through the centuries that the Enemy continues to sow seeds of doubt: *I know what the Bible says, but how do we know that is really, what God meant? Isn't it a matter of one's way of interpreting Scripture? Times have changed; can we say that the Bible applies to us today? Is it really wrong to covet what someone else has? Did God really say...?* Therefore, the questions, seeds of doubt about the Scriptures, continue. Do you recognize this line of questioning? If we, as born-again believers in Christ, begin to question the Bible, then we will neglect developing an intimate relationship with our Heavenly Father through the reading of His Word. Therefore, as we feed less and less on God's Word, and as truth is questioned more and more, we become insensitive—nonreactive to the sin in our own lives as well as all the sin in the world around us.

At this point, you might be thinking that I am very much a legalist, a Pharisee. You know what I mean—*if your hair's too long, there's sin in your heart* type of Christianity. Let me remind you what the Apostle Paul said concerning our Christian liberty: "But where sin abounded, grace abounded much more" (Galatians 5:20b, NKJV) and "What shall we say then? Shall we continue in sin that grace may abound? Certainly not!" (Galatians 6:1-2a, NKJV). No, I am not in any way presenting a *works salvation* or saying that we can do enough good to earn God's grace. On the contrary, God's grace is a free gift and is offered to everyone, and it is only because of His mercy that we are given the opportunity to be saved. We would all stand condemned except for His marvelous grace. However, many Christians have used the liberty they have in Christ as a license to sin because they have become insensitive to the leading of the Holy Spirit.

So many times, a person who has grown up in a legalistic home or church does not quite know how to handle their liberty in Christ once they finally break free. For these persons, the pendulum swings too far in the opposite direction. In order to prevent themselves from appearing judgmental, they compromise the truth and solid convictions that they had once endeared.

If you have this giant checklist of rules and regulations you attempt in your own strength to keep each day, you probably feel that the desensitization begins when one lays aside the guilt and shame of broken commandments for the healing of grace. Actually, you began to become desensitized to the power of the Holy Spirit the moment you formed the list of do's and don'ts and attempted, in your own power, to be *good*.

Thus, the pendulum swings from one extreme to the other. Whether someone is a legalist who feels that everything except what they prefer is to be viewed as sin, or someone uses their Christian freedom as a ticket to indulge in the most blatant sins, each has been desensitized. Both have abused God's grace in that they operate in the flesh. Both of these persons have become insensitive and nonreactive to the Holy Spirit—the legalist, desensitized to the power of the Holy Spirit—the liberal, desensitized to the meaning of walking circumspectly. Only the grace of God can bring that pendulum back to the center where things are viewed in proper perspective, where there is balance, and where we become sensitized instead of desensitized to the Holy Spirit's voice.

As for me, the only time I received spiritual food as a child was on Sundays, and that simply was not enough nourishment to prevent my being desensitized. Oh no, I was not without moral conscience. I understood the difference between right and wrong. The fact of the matter is that by the time I was in

Junior High School, I had become severely numbed, insensitive, to the Holy Spirit's voice. Deep down inside, I still had a desire to be different from the world, but because I was desensitized, my actions, my thoughts, and my choices in general had become just like the world.

Without disclosing too much of my past, let me say, from personal experience, that as you allow yourself to be desensitized you are imprisoning yourself. You will step into that prison cell, shut and lock the door behind you, and begin to, layer upon layer, paper the walls of that prison with the lies of the Enemy.

While I knew God's Word must be the final authority upon which everything in my life must be based, I did not have a clue about what the Bible had to say. Therefore, just as I described in the previous paragraph, I stepped into a prison of my own making. I felt trapped! I did not like the prison and I did not like myself! Too numb to hear what my Heavenly Father was saying, I was not growing closer to Him but was becoming more and more spiritually emaciated.

A very faulty belief system was emerging, and, although I hated myself for it, I began to live more like a child of the Devil than a child of the Lord God. For every right, godly action, three wrong, ungodly actions would be manifested in me. Every time I did or thought something that was wrong, I spent much time trying to reason, rationalize, and/or justify my actions. The Holy Spirit would convict me that certain things were wrong; I was miserable, but I continued to question: *What is wrong with...? What if...?* I was desensitized to the max! Sure, I would feel a minute twinge of guilt, which alerted me to the fact I was headed for trouble, but I had become so numb to *wrong* that I easily brushed the guilt aside.

We are instructed in Second Corinthians chapter thirteen verse five to "Examine yourselves *as to* whether you are in the faith" (verse 5a, NKJV). Examination of our actions, thoughts, and motives and the *whys* of those actions, thoughts, and motives is a necessary operation, which keeps us in check, spiritually.

If you had asked me if I knew that I had been saved, I would have immediately answered, "Yes." The truth of the matter: I constantly doubted. I had been desensitized by all the garbage I had allowed to enter, not only allowed but also deliberately put into, my heart and mind with the end result of having no joy, no peace, and doubts concerning my salvation.

There are some who have determined that if you ever doubt your salvation, it is because you have never truly trusted Christ. It is not my intention to split theological hairs, but I know from personal experience that you can be saved and be so far from your Heavenly Father that you doubt whether or not you have been saved.

"But the devil would never make you doubt because he does not want you to be saved," they say. My answer is, "EXACTLY!" If you have not been saved, had that drink of Living Water, then the Enemy will not cause you to question your salvation. On the other hand, if you truly are saved he wants to render you an unfruitful Christian. Let me remind you again

Satan is the master of deceit and doubt. Remember the Garden of Eden. If he can keep you in a constant state of confusion and doubt, he can rob you of your joy and peace of mind, and you will be ineffective as salt and light in this tasteless, dark world. In addition, the Holy Spirit will not cause you to be filled with doubts. Instead, if you are not saved, He will convict you of your need for Christ, the Savior. Many times, the reason for doubts concerning our salvation is the result of our not growing in our walk with Christ.

If I am really saved, then why do I consistently struggle with feelings of guilt? That, my friend, is a warning flag of the Holy Spirit telling you to turn around and go the opposite direction—LEAVE IT ALONE! Actually, you should thank the Lord that the Holy Spirit's conviction in your life has the power to cause those guilt feelings. If you will pay attention to these warnings and choose to be spiritually-minded instead of worldly-minded, you will be spared a lot of heartache.

Scientific fact: It is impossible for a person to think about two different things at the exact same moment. It is difficult for us to understand and accept this fact because thoughts fly so swiftly through our minds in rapid succession that we feel we are thinking about two things at the same time. In other words, a person cannot think on ungodly things and think on the things of Christ at the same time. Desensitization will not take place if we remain focused on Christ.

If you profess to know Christ, personally, please take the time for a spiritual check-up. We must guard our hearts and minds against things that are not conducive to our spiritual health. Heed this instruction from Proverbs: "[20]My son, pay attention to my words; listen closely to my sayings. [21]Don't lose sight of them; keep them within your heart. [22]For they are life to those who find them, and health to one's whole body. [23]Guard your heart above all else, for it is the source of life. [24]Don't let your mouth speak dishonestly, and don't let your lips talk deviously. [25]Let your eyes look forward; fix your gaze straight ahead. [26]Carefully consider the path for your feet, and all your ways will be established. [27]Don't turn to the right or to the left; keep your feet away from evil" (Proverbs 4:20-27, HCSB). It is quite difficult to guard your heart while allowing things to enter the gateways (eyes and ears) to your heart and mind that do not edify.

There is another way in which we can be desensitized to the truth. When we begin to question the truth of who we are in Christ Jesus, then we will soon begin to believe the lies that tell us we are not loved or that God only loves us when we are good, perfect. As we listen to the lies of the Enemy and spend less and less time in God's Word, we become insensitive to the Holy Spirit's speaking the truth of God's love and peace to us.

By the time I finished Junior High School, I did not know who I was in Christ. I felt so alone and unloved. At the age of thirteen, I became the victim of many shaming words and actions. I felt ashamed of *who* I was and *what* I thought I was. I felt dirty and, not only unloved but extremely unlovable. What did I do? Because I had been desensitized I did not seek truth, but instead, I went back to the well and picked up my water jar. That water jar contained the familiar and brought a certain amount of false comfort for a brief moment. I did not realize that picking up the water jar of my self-righteous works and means of gaining love and acceptance would only enslave me, carving a deep chasm between my loving Heavenly Father and me. Therefore, instead of leaving my water jar in the very capable hands of Jesus Christ, the author and perfecter of my faith, I picked it up and tried very hard to gain love and acceptance on my own.

In all probability, every one of us who name the name of Christ, have at some time been desensitized to the Holy Spirit, at least to a small degree. This process begins with a thought, a temptation, to compromise in some area of our lives. However, God is faithful, and He continues to convict us of particular things, which are not right in our lives. The time to turn around is when you feel the guilt, when you sense the conviction, before your senses are so dulled by the many distracting, as well as ungodly, things the world has to offer. Do not allow yourself to be desensitized to the Holy Spirit's voice, leading, guiding, and convicting in your life. Remember this children's song and obey its teaching:

Oh, be careful little eyes what you see.
Oh, be careful little eyes what you see,
For the Father up above is looking down in love.
Oh, be careful little eyes what you see.

Oh, be careful little ears what you hear.
Oh, be careful little ears what you hear,
For the Father up above is looking down in
love.
Oh, be careful little ears what you hear.

Oh, be careful little feet where you go.
Oh, be careful little feet where you go,
For the Father up above is looking down in
love.
Oh, be careful little feet where you go.

Oh, be careful little hands what you do.
Oh, be careful little hands what you do,
For the Father up above is looking down in
love.
Oh, be careful little hands what you do.

The woman at the well, however, did not yet have the Holy Spirit dwelling within her. Even though she was not a believer in the Messiah, Jesus Christ, I believe that Satan had employed this tactic of desensitization in attempts to prevent her ever placing her faith in Christ. It is quite possible that at sometime in adolescence she had gradually been desensitized to truth. Based upon her response in verse twelve of chapter four, it seems obvious that she had heard about God and acknowledged Jacob, whom God had chosen to be the father of His people, to be among her ancestors. No doubt, this woman had been taught about Jehovah God—the God of Abraham, Isaac, and Jacob, but through various circumstances and/

or conversations with people she trusted, she had become desensitized to the truth of who God is. We find her drawing water from a well, which she declares was given to the Samaritans by their father, Jacob, and yet she seems oblivious to the true significance of the well and the true Giver of the cool water that had quenched her thirst day after day. I do not know about you, but I must ask, "Why?" The most likely answer is she was desensitized to truth, until this particular day—this divine appointment—when she came face-to-face and eye-to-eye with Truth.

The bottom line is that it does not matter what instruments were employed in this process of desensitization. We all are faced with choices that must be made, and when we neglect time in the Word, we have chosen to allow ourselves to be desensitized to Truth. Many times, we get to the point we experience much difficulty in distinguishing between truth and lies. Therefore, as believers, we must steadfastly remain face-to-face and eye-to-eye with Truth, Jesus Christ, allowing Him to guide us and to be the final authority in everything we do, say, and think. If you have not yet been saved, it is not too late. Turn around and run to Jesus. He waits with open arms to show you truth and to place His sensitizing agent, the Holy Spirit, in your life.

Desensitized! It is the first step **down** the road to destruction. Do not let it happen to you!

CHAPTER THREE

Demoralized

Numbed—desensitized—confused! This blurring of the lines between right and wrong, holy and profane—that is what takes place when we become desensitized—can only lead to a life of guilt and shame.

Let us take a closer look at the life of the woman at the well in John chapter four. We do not know her name, but I hate to continue referring to her as *the woman at the well* as if she had no identity or as if she were a stone statue used to decorate the area surrounding the well. From now on, or at least in the next few chapters, I think I will give to her the name, Prisoner, for that perfectly describes her.

Somewhere along the line, perhaps in her childhood, she began to see things and hear things that began this desensitization process—a process that in a few short years would lead to her demoralization. No doubt, Prisoner grew up the same as most of the other girls around Sychar, but something happened that caused her thinking and her perception of self and the world around her to become twisted.

At this point would probably be a good time to examine the meaning of *demoralize* as is found in *Webster's New Dictionary of the English Language*:

- **demoralize** *vb* **1:** to corrupt in morals **2:** to weaken in discipline or spirit

In my opinion, the second definition of *demoralize* should be given first. More times than not, it has been seen that demoralization is a process that begins with a weakening in discipline or spirit. Satan begins to wear us down by constantly throwing out the many lures of sin, which abound everywhere. If we do not make a conscious effort to stay in the Word, we become weak. It is then that this weakening in discipline or spirit gives way to the corruption of morals as we compromise everything we know to be right. I believe this is probably what happened to Prisoner, the woman at the well.

Step into character, or perhaps I should say "*step into her sandals*," if you will and try to imagine for a moment what her life might possibly have been like. Because I, as well as many of you, have so much in common with Prisoner, perhaps we will have a clearer understanding of her if we bring her into our world. Although we are *worlds* apart, so to speak, some things, especially concerning human nature, are common to every age.

~~~~~~~~~~~~~~~

Prisoner and her best friend sat in the yard next to the stone fence simply talking as best friends do. As they talked, the subject of the latest movies, the top ten songs, and the hottest fashions came up. Prisoner's friend began to talk about the sensual images she had viewed on the movie screen so many times. She reached over, grabbed her iPod, and shared with Prisoner the new music selection that had just been downloaded.

The next day, Prisoner went to her friend's house again. Her friend's parents were visiting with a neighbor, so Prisoner and her friend were alone in the house. Her friend took a DVD from the tower of neatly stacked, alphabetized movie selections that stood beside the very large home theater system and loaded it in the DVD player. While viewing the movie, Prisoner had a strange feeling that she was doing something wrong, but her eyes remained fixed on the screen as if they were frozen in place. Common Sense told her to turn her eyes the other direction, but her lustful appetite won out and she continued to gaze intently at things she could have never imagined. Before she realized what was happening, the content of that DVD was burned on her mind's computer. Prisoner hurried home—she had many things to process in her mind.

A few days later, Prisoner was talking to her mother. Without thinking, Prisoner began to pour out the crux of the recent conversations with her best friend. She even told her mother about the, highly questionable, movie that she had viewed at her friend's house. Although her mother was not particularly pleased to hear what had captivated Prisoner's thoughts, she did not bother to give instruction or explain to her daughter the possible consequences resulting from filling her mind with the wrong things.

Prisoner admitted that she felt somewhat guilty about her excitement over the movie images that seemed to constantly play in her mind, but she could not seem to erase the scenes from her memory. She determined she must simply try harder not to think about the movies or the music that had infiltrated her thoughts. The more she tried to not think about the movies, which contained nudity, profanity, murder, and...(You name it—it was in there), the more she asked herself what was wrong with these things. *After all, if they were really so bad, wouldn't her friend's mom and dad prevent her friend from viewing such things and listening to such profane song lyrics?*

Just when she thought she had overcome this obsession with movie stars and rock stars, the overwhelming need to belong—fit in with the crowd—be accepted—would sweep through her from the inside out with a chilling sort of fear. She was fearful of continuing in this possibly destructive behavior, but she was more afraid of not *belonging*. Prisoner's friend made it all seem so innocent, and spoke about the movies and music in such a way that made Prisoner feel left out because she was not savvy to the latest happenings on the big screen, etcetera.

Soon she found herself in a fantasy world where she was as beautiful as the women on the movie screen and **everyone** loved her. At first, she very rarely engaged in this world of daydreams where everyone lives happily ever after, but her trips to fantasyland became more frequent as her sense of belonging and significance ebbed away. While Prisoner had convinced herself her motivation for continuing in this ungodly behavior was fueled only by her need to belong, deep down inside she was beginning to enjoy the feelings the movies and music brought to her *ho-hum* life.

More and more, Prisoner found herself feeling very confused and somewhat disconnected from family and friends. She even felt somewhat distanced from the girl that had been her very best friend since early childhood. Looking back, Prisoner realized it was about the time she entered the fifth grade that she began to lose all sense of belonging—belonging to the group at school—belonging to her family. It seemed there was no place for Prisoner to *fit-in* and just be *herself*, but how could she be *herself* when she was not sure exactly what that meant?

Although she was six months to a year younger than the other fifth-graders, she felt much older than her years. Maybe she felt older because of the several years that gaped between her and the youngest of the family. Maybe it was because she spent so much time with the oldest sibling. She was unable to identify the basis of her feelings, and this only added to her insecurities, feelings of inadequacy, and feelings of not belonging.

In many ways, her mother seemed to have problems allowing her to grow up, although she expected Prisoner to maintain adult responsibilities concerning chores around the house and her behavior in the marketplace of Sychar. Perhaps, it was at this time in her life that she began to question the purpose of her existence on planet Earth.

Although it is difficult to determine just where the dysfunction began, at some point Prisoner began to withdraw and found it difficult to engage in both casual and meaningful conversation. Somehow, she had received the message that she should not talk because nothing she could say would be of any importance. Her thoughts and feelings about things did not matter!

Very often, the people she thought should have loved her most only had words of discouragement to offer. Very often, she heard things such as the following: "You can't do that (meaning that she was incapable)! What's wrong with you? You will never amount to anything! Why can't you be like your brother or like your sister? Just be good!" While Prisoner's parents never spoke these hurtful words to her, they seemed to be oblivious to the pain bludgeoning her heart like a giant sledgehammer. Because neither her mom nor her dad was very demonstrative with their love, she felt rejected, unloved, and unwanted—by everyone.

Prisoner made it from Elementary School into Junior High School with excellent grades. She remained on the honor roll throughout Junior High, but experienced tremendous fear and anxiety—especially when she had to stand before the class to give an oral book report. I suppose this stemmed from the fact that she felt anything she had to say was unimportant and/or would be misunderstood.

Prisoner thought that if she worked very hard and had good grades she would be accepted and loved by everyone. Oh how she longed for the assurance that she was loved, and she thought the way to know she was loved was for everyone to notice how well she performed. The reason she worked so hard to achieve a minute amount of significance stemmed from the fact she could not remember ever hearing the words, "I love you," even from her parents. She longed to hear, "I love you," particularly from her mother!

As Prisoner grew more insecure, she often asked her mother, "Do you love me?" Her mother never gave a straightforward answer, but instead would say, "Would I wash your clothes and cook for you if I didn't? What do you think?" If only her mother had not asked that last question, *what do you think?* Of course, Prisoner would never express what she was really thinking for fear of being disrespectful, so she would paste her best fake smile on her lips, shrug her shoulders, and walk away to a private place where she could have a good cry.

In the summer just before beginning her freshman year of High School something dreadful happened. Prisoner was walking along a lonely road on her way home from her friend's house when she heard the slow, lumbering, clip-clop of a horse's hooves. She turned to see an older teenage boy that she knew riding a beautiful chestnut colored horse. The rider of the horse stopped beside of Prisoner and asked if she would like a ride home. Prisoner loved horses, and since she did not have a horse of her own, she grasped every opportunity that came her way to climb onto the back of a horse.

Whenever she was on the back of a horse, she felt so free with the wind blowing through her long dark hair. She felt as though she was in her own world where there were no hurts, and she was free from the pain of who she was, or at least, who she perceived herself to be. Riding horses and/or grooming the horses granted escape from the painful reality of her depression and deep emotional dysfunction. Perhaps, it was the feeling that she was understood and she could pour out the deepest, darkest secrets of her soul into a caring ear that could never dare repeat what was told them that provided the sweetest respite.

Then Prisoner, without thinking twice about the possible outcome of her choice, started to get on the horse behind its rider. The boy said, "No, get in front and you can hold the reins and guide the horse." Prisoner gladly accepted the offer and climbed onto the horse in front of the boy, taking the reins of the bridle in her hands anxious to show off her riding skills.

As they rode along, she struggled to carry on casual conversation with the boy. She felt so awkward trying to think of something to say that would not sound stupid or that would not appear too forward. Prisoner, although unable to see the boy's face, began to sense a change in his attitude. At first, she thought she must have said something offensive that caused this sudden shift in the boy's attitude, but then decided it was only her imagination.

Unexpectedly, the boy began to whisper into Prisoner's ear. "You are very pretty, and stacked nicely for a thirteen-year-old." Of course, these words were somewhat flattering, but they also struck a note of fear in Prisoner's heart. She spurred the horse to speed him up to a canter in hopes of hurrying home before anything worse happened.

The boy reached his left hand around the left side of Prisoner's waist, took hold of the reins and pulled the bridle's bit back against the corners of the horse's mouth. "Whoa! There's no hurry." He left the reins in Prisoner's hands and began to fondle her small breasts. "Not bad for a girl of only thirteen," the boy smirked. She held tightly to the reins with one hand while trying to pry the boy's left hand away from her breasts with the other. "Please stop," she desperately pleaded. The boy only laughed and began to fondle her breasts more with his left hand while rubbing her right thigh with his right hand, pulling and tugging at her clothes attempting to do more than just touch the top her thigh.

"Stop," she shrieked, "or I will tell everyone what kind of person you are!"

"No one will believe you—you little whore. Everyone talks about how easy you are," he sneered.

Prisoner struggled so hard and was screaming so loudly that the horse was spooked and jerked his head from side to side. At this, the boy became very angry and knocked Prisoner off the horse and to the ground. "Don't you know anything about horses? You are so stupid," he yelled! "Remember this, if you tell anyone about what happened, I will kill you in such a manner it will look like suicide," he said with a wickedly convincing glare.

Prisoner stood to her feet, very shakily brushing the dirt from her clothes but then collapsed to a heap on the side of the road, sobbing uncontrollably. A myriad of emotions—hatred of the boy, guilt, shame, disgust for self, confusion, and fear—poured from the crucible of her soul and flooded over her, racing through her from head to foot and from foot to head. The boy's threat to kill her if she told anyone left her paralyzed with fear; she was convinced that he would be true to his word concerning this matter.

However, it was the boy's statements attacking her character—her innocence—her purity that inflicted the deepest wounds, causing Prisoner's emotions to spin completely out of control. *Why would anyone call me such a terrible name, a whore? What basis could anyone have to say that I am "easy?"* It was true there was a boy she liked and who had accompanied her to the church on Mt. Gerizim a few times, but they had never even been alone. Since he had always been the perfect gentleman toward Prisoner, it did not seem probable that he would have made such detrimental statements to anyone, especially to the boy who molested her because they despised one another.

Uncertain of what to do, she again stood to her feet, dried her tears, and started for home with thoughts of whether or not she should tell anyone racing through her mind. She determined that she must not let anyone know she had been crying; this revelation would bring too many unpleasant questions—questions Prisoner felt she could not answer or deal with.

Upon entering her house, she noticed her mother was in the kitchen preparing dinner. *Oh, good*, Prisoner thought, *I can bathe my face and change clothes before Mother notices anything*. She quickly bathed her face and eyes in hopes of relieving the redness and puffiness caused from the many tears, changed her clothes, and put the dirty clothes in to wash. Prisoner concluded that she must not tell anyone what had happened. Instead, she must try to be smarter in order to prevent her being molested again.

I suppose it was at this particular point in time that Prisoner's skills of deception were enhanced. When she was asked about her swollen, red eyes she said that her allergies were responsible, and when asked why she decided to wash her clothes that evening, she said she wanted to wear the same thing the next day. Thus, she embarks upon a life filled with deceit and mistrust of everyone.

Prisoner needed to tell someone, but whom could she tell? Who would believe that a thirteen-year-old girl was sexually molested? You see, the general consensus was that if a young child was molested, it was such a tragedy, but if a teenager was molested, they asked for it. Where could she go? Who would provide a fortress of safety and love for Prisoner?

Her mother would never believe her. This fact had been proven a month earlier while at the Sychar County Fair. Prisoner's mother had taken her and her younger sister to the fair. Her mother sat in the grandstands watching the show while Prisoner and her sister walked the midway and rode the exciting rides. While walking through the midway, they saw a neighbor boy and his girlfriend. They exchanged "hellos" as Prisoner and her sister hurried to the next ride. The neighbor boy went to the grandstands and told Prisoner's mother that she had left the fair with a boy.

When it came time to leave the fair, Prisoner's mother gave her quite a tongue-lashing. Although Prisoner insisted the neighbor had told a lie, her mother would not believe her. Prisoner's sister insisted the neighbor was telling a lie, but their mother said, "You've got to stop trying to cover-up for your sister."

Prisoner went home from the fair that evening in a state of total confusion. She knew that the neighbor had lied to her mother. In addition, she knew she had done nothing wrong. However, she felt over-whelmingly guilty, or was it shame that she was experiencing?

Prisoner needed to be loved and to know her life had some significance. She knew her life had not always been in such shambles, so searching the recesses of her soul in an attempt to recall something that had brought her comfort in the past she began to remember days when she was much younger. All of her performance-driven attempts to satisfy her thirst for love and purpose—always eating everything on her plate, trying to be sweet and kind, and trying to please everyone all of the time—Prisoner had stuffed into her water jar and put it away for safe keeping.

In the water jar was everything that had brought her comfort before, but the things that had once brought comfort for brief, fleeting moments had also failed her so many times. Nevertheless, Prisoner was desperate and did not know of anything else to do, so she diligently searched for the water jar. Once she found the water jar, she picked it up to examine its contents in hopes of finding something to medicate her pain, at least for a little while. Although it was somewhat larger than she remembered, it did contain the **familiar** things that had once given her affirmation—work your head off to be good. *Perform well and everyone will be happy—most importantly, you will be loved*, Prisoner thought.

With every tightening turn of the *vise-grip* on her heart, she felt compelled to try harder, perform better—reach a level of perfection. Prisoner's grades dropped drastically, adding to her frustration. Feeling isolated from friends, especially her best friend, Prisoner determined that if only she tried harder, did more good things, was a good little girl, that she could gain approval and acceptance, somehow erasing the shame of the molestation. It was extremely important to her that others think well of her. In this way, Prisoner could have some sense of accomplishment, significance, and a feeling of being loved.

She became very active in her church, which was located on Mt. Gerizim. Prisoner threw herself with reckless abandon into all kinds of good deeds such as staying in the nursery, bringing a devotional, and doing secretarial work for the Vacation Bible School; she even played one of the musical instruments. Oh, surely everyone would take notice of how many fruit baskets she helped to deliver to the shut-ins! None of these things, however, could ease the pain in Prisoner's heart, for the more she tried to gain a healthy sense of self-worth, the more she felt like a failure.

Thinking back to the time when she was in the early years of elementary school brought good memories that seemed only to melt away into the painful reality of her present state of mind. When she was a little girl, life was so simple.

Prisoner was an excellent student as a youngster, and even though she had always been somewhat shy, she considered everyone in her class to be a friend, and they all considered her their friend. Just friends. She did not have problems with relationships then— but that time of her life seemed so distant, almost as though it was an entire lifetime ago.

This is the way it was back then for Prisoner, but now somehow things began to be all distorted in her mind. The harder she tried to fit-in with the crowd, and the more she tried to *do good things*, the more isolated she felt. Perhaps Prisoner had heard it said, "You'll never amount to anything," just one too many times. Her morale had completely faded away into the hopelessness of her miserable life because she had been demoralized by so much negative talk and shamed by the molestation. Unfortunately, Prisoner began to sink to the depths of despair as depression crept into her life, overshadowing her like a heavy, black fog.

But wait! Children and young teens were not allowed to be depressed, not in Sychar anyway. Depression was a thing reserved for the elite adults who could afford the risks of being referred to as lazy and/or incompetent. Kids on the other hand, were never depressed or sad, but instead they just needed to try harder to be happy with the status quo. This was the general consensus around Sychar, anyway.

Nonetheless, Prisoner was experiencing a weakening in spirit and discipline, and as a result, found it more and more difficult to concentrate on her studies. She tried very hard to bring up her grades but was unable to do so because of physical exhaustion, which so much of the time accompanies depression, and because of her constant feelings of isolation. Naturally, the poor grades only compounded her feelings of worthlessness. Prisoner was trapped in a vicious whirlwind of confusion, swiftly spinning round and round but going nowhere.

It is difficult to determine just where, when, and how Prisoner began to suffer this demoralization. It just happened! Well, it did not really just happen. It was a gradual process—just another step down her spiral staircase that was leading nowhere except to the pit of enslavement. Yes, it can be safely assumed the demoralization and depression were a very gradual occurrence—so gradual an occurrence that by the time Prisoner realized something was wrong, she felt there was no escape from the chains that held her fast.

By this time in her young life, she was experiencing relational difficulties. Prisoner watched as the other teens conversed and related to each other as friends to friends. The girls were able to talk to guys and guys to girls just as friends. She longed to have the capacity to simply be able to talk to others, but somehow this simple pleasure eluded her. Prisoner had enough trouble just talking to the other girls in her class, how could she ever talk to a member of the opposite sex? Besides, since the molestation she did not think there was anyone who could be trusted. She began to feel everyone had ulterior motives and was out to *get* her.

Because of the exhaustion caused from the depression, Prisoner did not realize that she was paralyzed by fear. She had always been quite independent and felt as though she could handle any situation that might arise. At least, this is the way she had been before the molestation.

There was never any rest for Prisoner as any few moments of sleep she was afforded were constantly interrupted with hellish nightmares of her perpetrator. Night after night, she was jolted from her sleep by the violent kicking of her legs, her body drenched in a cold sweat. "Fear" cannot adequately describe what Prisoner experienced; the dreams seemed so real, as though her molester was right there in her bedroom reaching under the covers sliding his hands up and down her legs.

The very next summer, now at the age of four-teen, Prisoner, her mother, and her younger sister were again at the county fair. This time, her mother had come down from the grandstands and ventured into the midway. Prisoner found her mother standing in front of the Tunnel of Horrors talking with the preacher from a nearby town. It is ironic that they were standing in front of the Tunnel of Horrors because that is exactly what it turned out to be for Prisoner.

Evidently, the preacher had asked Prisoner's mother to ride with him through the Tunnel of Horrors, and she had refused. Prisoner's arrival on the scene provided an easy *out* for her mother, as she insisted Prisoner would be happy to ride with the preacher. No doubt, Prisoner's mother thought it would not look good for a married woman to ride with a man other than her husband, but that no one would think anything about a young girl riding with a married man. After all, this man was a preacher. Prisoner felt humiliated, but even though she displayed reluctance to do so, she obeyed her mother.

Although the ride only lasted two and one-half to three minutes, it seemed like an eternity. As the preacher forced Prisoner's head against his shoulder, a million questions flooded her mind: *How can I get out of here? What can I do? I'm a pretty good fighter; should I punch his lights out? Don't the Scriptures say something about not touching God's man? What is my mother trying to do to me by forcing me to ride with this man?*

Fortunately, nothing more happened than the preacher's forcing Prisoner's head against his shoulder as he kissed her forehead. Unfortunately, however, this act against Prisoner left her filled with more shame. Although it was not the preacher who had molested her, what he had done coupled with the molestation, which happened the year before, and had continued sporadically into this year, caused Prisoner to feel, not only unloved, but also very dirty.

Not only did Prisoner feel worthless, but she also felt she was defective in some way. *There must be something wrong with me*, she thought, *or these things would not have happened. If my mother really loved me, why would she have deliberately placed me in such a situation? Maybe the molestation really was my fault...* and so the questions and feelings of shame, worthlessness, fear, confusion, and inadequacy skyrocketed.

Her world really began to fall apart when she was a junior in High School. She began to notice her best and only friend did not want to spend as much time with Prisoner as she once did. To make matters worse, the boy she had dated for the past few months broke off the relationship and would not even speak to her. The boy's cousin came to Prisoner and told her the reason for the sudden breakup: "I'm sorry to be the one to tell you this," his cousin told her, "but the only reason he went out with you is because some of the other guys made a bet with him. They bet him he couldn't score with you, but he's so hung-up on himself he thought you would be another notch in his belt, so to speak. Since he lost the bet he doesn't want to have anything else to do with you."

Prisoner knew a boy like this would only cause her much grief, but still she felt an overwhelming sense of abandonment at losing both her best friend and her boyfriend. *There really is something wrong with me. I am no good! I'll bet my friends found out about the molestation that's been going on for almost three years.* With these thoughts constantly occupying her mind, she clung to the **false hope** that the **familiar** things from her water jar would ease her pain and give her the security of love her heart had yearned for through the years.

Like a clever spider, the lies she had believed were spinning an intricate web of deception in her mind that kept her enslaved in the frustration that comes from working hard to please others in hopes she would somehow find affirmation and acceptance. Prisoner was unable to comprehend that things she had used in the past to supposedly bring meaning and purpose to her life were, in actuality, holding her in shackles.

She sometimes had difficulty distinguishing between reality and fantasy. For the past three to four years, she had felt disconnected from family and friends, but now she sensed a degree of disconnectedness from self. At times, she felt as though she was watching herself from a distance—nothing seemed real.

It is odd how the things we hate can become a part of us in such a short period of time. Why is it that shame always yields to more and more sin? It does, and this proved true in Prisoner's life. Prisoner was shamed by the molestation and the event with the preacher. She experienced more shame because of the perceived rejection by her best friend and boyfriend, but still she gave way to a very promiscuous lifestyle. Perhaps it was her desperate need for love that drove her to constantly make such poor choices, and although she hated herself because of her ungodly actions, she kept making the same mistakes over and over again. She went looking for love in all the wrong places, in all the wrong ways, and from all the wrong people. Maybe the fact her perpetrator was a trusted family member wreaked such havoc on her emotions that she began to equate this with love. Yes, her morals had become corrupt, so most of her years at Sychar High School were spent living in a vicious cycle of shame—sin—guilt—turning over a new leaf—shame—sin—guilt—turning over a new leaf…

There was a brief period of time during her senior year of high school that she was able to lay aside her water jar with all of its false hopes and securities. Prisoner met a very devout young man who asked her out on a date. He was like no other young man she had ever known. Beginning and ending each date with prayer and/or a study of the Scriptures was very refreshing, but for someone like Prisoner, it also sent a slight shockwave of confusion through her emotions. However, for a very brief, but sweet moment, she laid down her water jar, which contained all her performance-oriented searching for love and meaning of life.

~~~~~~~~~~~~~~~

Please hear me out on this before you write me off as a heretic. I know the dangers of *adding to* and/or *taking away from* the Scriptures, and I would never intentionally, knowingly do that. Nevertheless, I believe through probing, studying, and dissecting the Scriptures we can begin to make some specula- tions whereby we understand the *why's* of Prisoner's (the woman at the well) destructive behaviors. I mean, have you not ever wondered what her child- hood was like, why she encountered such difficulty in relationships with men, or what possible series of events helped to shape her perspective? How can we learn from this woman if we do not question and speculate about the information that John gives us in this passage?

While I can only study the Word and specu- late concerning this woman's demise, I know from personal experience people do not just suddenly one day decide to totally wreck their lives. Instead, it is a gradual process of skewed rationalization that leads to one poor choice after another. In other words, the woman at the well in John chapter four did not wake up one day in adulthood and decide: "Okay, I think I should have as my life's ambition to go from one bad relationship to another—make a mess of my life— feel trapped, miserable, defeated, and depressed. Oh, that sounds like such fun!" Now, that line of thinking *is* completely and utterly ridiculous!

No, this was not the case. I believe at some point she had become desensitized to what is right and wrong—not that she had no conscience, but she, like us, began to question, "What's wrong with a little idolatry on the side, etcetera?" This could have simply been due to the fact that she was a Samaritan—partially of Jewish ancestry and partially of Assyrian ancestry.

Whatever the reason and by whatever means, there was a time, probably in childhood, in which she was confronted with things that caused her to question God and/or His existence. We can be certain she questioned the truth or trustworthiness of the Scriptures. Once she was desensitized to truth, then Satan was able to employ his next strategy—demoralization.

Of course, we understand from this passage of Scripture that she had been demoralized because she was obviously living a morally corrupt lifestyle. If her only problem had been she was widowed five times, and had not conceded to an immoral lifestyle, I do not believe Jesus would have mentioned this fact as a means of confronting her with the issue of her sin.

Whether or not she had experienced some type of shaming devastation or shame-based messages, is sheer speculation, but speaking from a fountain of personal experience, I believe that is probably what happened. Most people do not give way to immorality without first experiencing weakening in discipline or spirit. Therefore, I believe she must have been the victim of some shameful event or perhaps, just shame-based messages that caused her to feel inadequate and/or defective in some way.

I asked a state-board licensed, certified counselor, "How do unresolved issues from childhood affect adult behaviors?" Here is what she had to say concerning the possible digressive process of events that brought this woman to the point of demoralization:

"One thing about unresolved issues has to do with the way the Enemy (the devil) uses them as weapons. I will use the example of my having been molested as a child. Any time a child is molested, whether the molestation is severe or a one or two time incident, the affects can be far reaching.

"Variables such as whether it was a trusted friend or family member versus a stranger or peer, the age of the child, etcetera, can determine the affects and manifestations. For some it may mean that they have difficulty trusting while for others they become too trusting. Some may want nothing to do with sex, while others may become promiscuous. Some become very controlling, or codependent, or easily manipulated.

"The bottom line is that there is something that the Enemy is using to keep them from God. For example, I later came to realize that I was promiscuous because my molestation was somehow translated in my mind as love—the way to feel that I was wanted and worthwhile. However, all the while the Enemy was trapping me and leading me further from the light."

This counselor further elaborated that, based on this woman's poor relationship choices it is very likely she may have been shamed. "Shame says, 'there is something wrong with me' as opposed to

'I have done something wrong,' which is guilt. Of course, women of that day were most often treated as property and sometimes less cared for than the animals, so that, too, may have had a great impact on her life." It is my opinion this view of women was, in and of itself, a very shaming message.

In retrospect of my own growing-up years, I have come to realize for the most part, I lived with depression and anxiety. I have also come to realize that my depression and disconnectedness was because I grew up in a shame-based family system. Please, understand I am not blaming anyone but myself for my many poor choices in life, but when a person believes the lies that result in shame, depression is many times the result. Whether all of the messages I received were actually shame-based messages or it was only that my perception of things was all wrong, I am not sure. However, I had many feelings of inadequacy, as though I never could quite measure-up—even as a young child.

Then there were messages, which could or could not have been shame-based, but that I interpreted as being shameful. For example: I was born the fourth of five children. The first three children, two girls and a boy, are separated in age by approximately two years between each. However, there are five years separating my brother, the last of the first three children, and me. I was born before the days of ultrasounds, but judging from my heartbeat, the doctor vowed and declared my mother would have another son. Many times throughout my childhood and teenage years I heard, "You were supposed to be a boy. The doctor thought sure you would be a boy." I also heard my mother say many times she always wanted another boy.

Therefore, the Enemy used those words to cause me to feel ashamed that I was a girl. No, I never developed any same-sex attractions because of this, but I did feel unwanted and unloved. I do not believe my mother intended to hurt me or cause me shame with these words, but that the Enemy used this as a means to distract me from the **truth** of God's love for me. I felt that if I was unwanted and unloved by my biological family, then God did not want or love me. Oh sure, I knew God loved me enough to save me, but I viewed that as a collective love—"God so loved the **world**." As for a sense of belonging and acceptance, it was years before I realized that to God I am valuable.

Because my family was very performance-oriented, I learned early in life that the way to gain acceptance, approval, and love was to perform well enough. However, it is impossible for anyone to perform well enough on a consistent basis, and the devastation of this failure only added to the shameful feelings that there was something wrong with me.

Although I had always thought of myself as being extremely independent, I now understand I was not independent, but instead, I was isolated. In fact, in order to cope with the isolation I convinced myself I could operate independently and that I did not need anyone, but I was actually very easily manipulated and intimidated. If someone threw a little intimidation my way, he/she could talk me into doing almost anything.

Yes, it began with my being desensitized, and then through shame I was demoralized. Although I longed for love and acceptance to no avail, it was the immorality that created the dark clouds of despair—wrapping the chains of imprisonment around me, choking the very life out of me. "Why?" Charles Stanley put it this way: "The root of every sin can be traced directly to a true basic human need that we have chosen to meet in our way instead of God's way."

No doubt, an entire volume could be written by expounding on the quote of Charles Stanley, but that will have to be put aside until a later time. Right now, I want to talk with you heart-to-heart. Are you a prisoner of your past sins? Have you been demoralized in some way? Perhaps, your morals were corrupt at one time and now you no longer live that way, but the darkness of your past continues to haunt you. I am here to tell you that you can be free! Confess your sins—Christ will forgive and cleanse you (1John 1:9).

It is important that we do not cling to a victim mentality, but that we, instead, confess our sin by its name. Why? Because, although we may have experienced shame and truly been victimized in some way, ultimately we make the choices for right behaviors or wrong behaviors. Continuing to *pass the buck* and blame others and/or circumstances for our sin is one of the primary ways in which Satan keeps us enslaved by the guilt of sins God has already forgiven.

Too many times, we ask Christ to forgive us and then we blurt out this disclaimer: "Lord, please forgive me for living in immorality, **but** You know I did those things because I felt so unlovely. I just needed to be loved." On the other hand, there are times when we are not truly sorry we have sinned, but only sorry we were caught and had to suffer the consequences of that sin.

As for myself, I literally spent most of my adult life begging God to forgive me for things I had already asked Him to forgive hundreds of times prior. My belief system was so warped from choosing to believe the Enemy's lies that I clung to the false hope that if I begged long enough and diligently enough God would forgive me. I simply could not get past my past!

On the other hand, if you have asked God to forgive you, but have, at the same time, made excuses for why you did certain things, you might be surprised to find how freeing it is to own up to your wrongdoings. If you have confessed your sins, owning what you have done, then rest in His forgiveness. To quote the counselor I referenced earlier in this chapter: "I believe in order for me to feel the full weight of God's forgiveness and grace, I had to own the full weight of what I had done—the choice I had made. Until I had done that, there was a piece held back from God, which affected my testimony and my ministry."

You do not have to remain demoralized. Place all your sins on Jesus—He can handle it, and His grace is sufficient to set you free!

CHAPTER FOUR

Destitute

"Water, water everywhere, nor any drop to drink…." (*The Rhyme of the Ancient Mariner,* Samuel Taylor Coleridge). I can remember reading this piece of literature and finding myself thoroughly exhausted and extremely thirsty.

Have you ever been so thirsty you felt as though you would die if you did not get a drink of water very soon? Then again, have you ever been so thirsty that once you finally got a drink of water, it just did not taste right, and you were not satisfied? I recall one trip Terry, the kids, and I took to Florida. We went in the early part of August, and it was really hot and dry. After a day and a half in the hot Florida sun and the consumption of too many sodas, I began to feel like the *ancient mariner*. I sat there looking at the ocean or swimming in it, and felt as though I would collapse if I did not get a drink of water. Every place we went to eat, I would order water to drink, but it did not quench my thirst. Furthermore, it tasted awful and smelled even worse.

Obviously, I survived the ordeal. However, there is another kind of thirst, and if it is not quenched according to God's plan for us, it will leave us destitute. *Strategy number three—***destitution**! According to the dictionary, the word *destitute* means lacking something needed or desired. I want to focus on the lack, absence, of something needed rather than on the lack of something desired. While the lack of something desired, something we want, may cause a degree of pain or emptiness, there is no aching of soul comparable to the pain caused from the deprivation of a true need.

So many times when we hear of someone being destitute, we automatically think of the homeless person on the street who scavenges the garbage cans looking for food, sleeps under bridges, overpasses, and/or on park benches, and uses newspaper to insulate their bodies from the cold. However, while a person destitute of the needs of food, clothing, and shelter truly experience the degradation of their demise, there is another type of destitution—destitution that is not as obvious as that of the homeless person. I am referring to being destitute of spirit—the kind of dryness of soul that makes every facet of life seem like you are continuously walking through a desert.

Can you see that the woman at the well was suffering from destitution? What was the cause of her dilemma? What happened to leave her as dry as the dusty Palestinian roads, which met the soles of her sandals each day? Before we continue any further with this line of questioning, let us step back and probe deeper into the saga of Prisoner that was begun in the last chapter.

~~~~~~~~~~~~~~~

Yes, for a brief moment Prisoner laid aside the water jar with all of the junk from her past, which she had managed to cram into it. At last, she thought she had found someone who would truly love her just because of the qualities of character she possessed.

There was a major problem concerning this newfound love—Prisoner's thinking was so twisted she did not recognize real love when it came her way. Perhaps this inability to receive love as well as give love was attributable to the lingering affects of the molestation and other shame-filled events of her young life. In her way of thinking, love was a great emotional high, which could only be demonstrated through physical measures. Although she had never actually engaged in sexual activity, she far exceeded the boundaries of the law that she attempted to employ to govern her life. Because the young man who stepped into her life was a perfect gentleman and had not even attempted nor asked permission to kiss her, Prisoner felt he did not really love her.

Prisoner tried, more diligently than ever, to be good and prove herself worthy of this man's attentions. Everyday she opened the Scriptures; however, it was not for the benefit of knowing God and drawing closer to Him. She was only trying to impress this young man and prove her value to both God and him.

While the young man had proposed marriage and Prisoner had accepted, she did not feel he really loved her so the engagement was short-lived. Finally, one day it happened. Continuing to feel unloved and very unlovable, she went back and picked up her water jar in search of love and significance. Once she found it, she noticed how much larger it was compared to the last time she had picked it up. She kept reminding herself that everything she had tried before, all of her *good-girl-things*, had failed in bringing lasting satisfaction, but her overwhelming need to know she was loved and wanted won out and she clung to the water jar with all of her might.

Before the end of Prisoner's senior year of High School, another young man had stepped into her life. While this young man was not the devout saint the former young man was, he was a gentleman and truly cared for Prisoner. They enjoyed many of the same hobbies such as swimming, horseback riding, and sports. Prisoner thought she had found the love of her dreams, although when it came to sharing from her heart and discussing things of real importance her lips were tightly sealed.

Graduation Day came at last. As Prisoner began getting dressed for the graduation exercises, her thoughts drifted back over the past four years, but more recently to the problems she experienced in her senior English class. That class had been one big chaotic nightmare for her, and at one point, she was afraid she would not pass the course; however, Prisoner managed to narrowly pass the course.

The problems with her senior English class began with the writing of a one-page composition on Greek Mythology. The class was instructed to choose one myth, tell about the myth, and then give the logical explanation for the myth. Prisoner followed the instructions, or so she thought, and handed her paper to the teacher. She was devastated when the teacher returned her paper to her with the grade of "F" written at the top of the page in bright red ink.

Short compositions were the one thing at which Prisoner had always excelled. Since there were no marks indicating grammatical errors on her paper she asked her teacher why she had received a failing grade. The teacher replied, "You did not do what you were told to do," and then she added, "I will allow you to rewrite the paper and turn it in tomorrow." Still not certain of what she had done wrong, Prisoner asked one of the other girls in the class if she could read her paper. After reading this girl's paper, she was still uncertain of what was wrong with her composition.

That afternoon she went home and rewrote the paper three times before settling on which of the papers to turn in the next day. Besides changing some of the words and restructuring a few sentences, she felt there was nothing else that could be done to improve the composition; after all, she had written the paper in the same manner as everyone else in the class.

The next morning Prisoner dashed off to school. She hoped and prayed during the entire six-mile trip that this paper on Greek Mythology, which would be in her teacher's hand in approximately twenty minutes, would be rewarded with a "C" grade, or, at the very least, a passing grade of "D". The remainder of the day at school was a tiring, stressful experience, and that night at home did not prove to be any better. She was not afforded very much rest that night; she kept waking up every thirty to forty-five minutes thinking of her composition and hoping the teacher might possibly have mercy on her.

When she arrived in her English class the next day, the teacher handed to Prisoner the one-page composition on Greek Mythology. At the top of the page in bright red ink was her grade—a zero. Prisoner approached the teacher after class and said, "I don't understand…" Before she could complete the sentence, the teacher snapped back, "That's right; you don't understand! There are many things you don't understand. I gave you a chance to make-up this grade, but you refused to do as you were instructed! There is nothing more to be said!"

To make matters worse, the school's guidance counselor stopped Prisoner in the hall and asked her why she had refused to do her homework. When Prisoner explained to him the entire situation, he replied, "I'm sorry this happened, but there is really nothing I can do about it. It is your word against the teacher's word, and as unfortunate as it is, the teacher is always right."

Although Prisoner was hurt and humiliated over her grade, she had come to believe she was destined for such unfortunate, unfair circumstances. She began fretting over the fact that the two grades she had received for her composition on Greek Mythology could possibly cause her to fail senior English. Prisoner knew she could not count on test scores to pull her grades up enough for her to pass the course. After all, she had experienced *test anxiety* since the seventh grade. Test anxiety, feelings of isolation and disconnectedness, along with the feeling that this was her destiny resulted in her never being able to focus long enough to study for a test.

Prisoner immediately began thinking about what she could do in the event she failed this required course of study—English Composition. She felt she had few options. One, she could consider Summer School, but that would mean added cost she did not have. Prisoner knew her parents did not have the money for Summer School; she also knew her parents would insist that she go back to Sychar High School and repeat her senior year.

In Prisoner's way of thinking, repeating her senior year at Sychar High School was absolutely out of the question. This would be too humiliating, and she felt she had already suffered more than her share of shame. The only other option Prisoner felt she had was to run away from home if she failed and could not graduate. For the remaining six weeks of school before graduation, she tried to figure out where she would run to and how she could manage to make a living for herself without a high school diploma.

At last, the nightmare was over. Managing to receive a passing grade in senior English, Prisoner was now finished with school, at least for one year.

She had decided to work for a year before entering college, although she did not know if she would be accepted into a college with such poor grades. In any case, Prisoner needed some time away from the educational system for she carried nothing but hurtful memories away from Sychar High School.

The night she graduated High School, the second young man who had stepped into her life asked her to be his wife. She gladly accepted and they were married shortly after.

Prisoner was a very emotionally unhealthy girl. What could someone of such extreme poverty bring to a marriage relationship? She had nothing to offer but the contents of her water jar—shame, hurt, confusion, depression, and anger. These things did not even come close to satisfying her longings for love and significance. What things to heap upon a new husband who carried around enough baggage of his own!

The marriage hit rough waters from the very outset of the voyage. Because Prisoner was seemingly so strong and independent on the outside, yet filled with so many insecurities on the inside, she was incapable of giving love, and she did not know what it meant to receive love either. Unsurprisingly, the marriage did not sail through the rough waters, but quickly fell apart on the large rocks of mistrust, insecurities, and unreal, unmet expectations.

One night, Prisoner found it difficult to sleep because of the questions and uncertain emotions that continually flooded her mind. She decided to go outside, thinking perhaps at night while the city was asleep and quiet she would be able to sort through these questions. It was a lovely night, and the large, beautiful, full moon showered the flower garden with a mist of silver spray. However, she was unmoved by this awesomely stunning sight.

Just a few short years before she would have, not only appreciated such a beautiful sight but also, basked in the beauty of how the silver beams shimmered through her long dark hair. Prisoner's thinking had become so shrouded with dark despair that it seemed nothing of any beauty could penetrate the perceived ugliness of her life.

She was uncertain of what to do next. Thoughts of returning to the home where she had grown up crept through her mind but soon vanished as she convinced herself she was neither welcome nor loved when she lived at home. Why should she think things would be any different this time? She even thought that perhaps now she could finally go to college, but soon dismissed the thought as fear of the unknown and depression took over. One thing was for certain, Prisoner could not continue to live in the house she had occupied with her first husband.

Prisoner was extremely lonely, and in spite of the turmoil of the relationship, she missed being married. Perhaps she missed preparing meals for a husband, or the occasional conversation between her and her husband that dispelled her loneliness for a brief time. I suppose Prisoner even missed the physical intimacy of marriage, although there were times when she loathed having to give in to her husband's wishes. She knew it was right and good to give herself to her husband, but in the back of her mind were flashbacks of the molestation, which sent fear, mistrust, and resentment riveting through her very soul. Unstable cannot begin to describe Prisoner's life, and it seemed the relentless emotional rollercoaster she was riding would never end.

From Prisoner's point of view, there was only one thing left to do. She must start anew—begin a new relationship—marry again—find someone who will love her. In the midst of her excitement, she paused and thought, *Because of the fact I've already gone through one bad marriage, it may be difficult to find someone who will love me enough to marry me.*

Once again, she turned to the **false** comfort of her water jar, and began recklessly fumbling through the trash that filled the water jar. Diligently searching for something to satisfy her need for love, she was determined to find a man who would meet her needs. If Prisoner was ever going to find a new husband, she knew she must become more social—go out into the city where she could meet people, particularly men. The thought, however, of forcing herself to become more of a social creature terrified her.

Prisoner felt she must have some means of drawing attention to herself without letting anyone see the pain and disgust that, in her manner of thinking, defined who she was. Looking deeper into her water jar, she painfully recalled the few words of praise that, as a child, had made its way into her hearing, giving her the attention she desperately craved—*"Prisoner has such a healthy appetite. We can always depend on her to eat everything on her plate. There are very few foods that she refuses to eat."* Weighing too much had never been a problem for Prisoner, so any time she felt she needed to be praised or needed attention she would eat enormous amounts of food.

Well, cleaning her plate at every meal had worked when she was a young girl, there was no reason it should not work now. After all, eating is a social thing; at the center of good fellowship is a good meal. Therefore, it happened that Prisoner gorged herself from one end of Samaria to the other, astounding everyone with her ability to eat so much food without the consequences of tremendous weight gain. Oh yes, she finally felt significant because of the attention she was receiving, and before long a man asked her to marry him.

At the altar for the second time, she was more determined than ever to make this marriage last. Prisoner continually reminded herself the only way this marriage would last, was if she always pleased her husband. In order to please him, she must never express her true feelings about anything, especially if her feelings and/or opinions were potentially controversial. Day in and day out, she tried very hard to be everything her husband wanted.

Prisoner soon realized the *good-little-girl* things that supposedly had worked in the past to give her a sense of value had turned into some extremely destructive behaviors. Any time she needed affirmation, she ate extremely large amounts of food. She ate and ate as if to say, *"Look at me. Don't you think I'm a good little girl? Please, give me some attention!"* However, this measure was not working any longer, and she could not control her appetite. Husband number two became disgusted with Prisoner's enormous appetite, in spite of her outward beauty. It became obvious the roots of this marriage sprang from the soil of burning lusts. When the fire of these burning desires became only smoldering embers, Prisoner and her husband decided to throw in the towel and call it quits.

Here she is again—alone, unloved, and still the victim of destitution. Prisoner had heard it said that it is impossible to survive without hope, and her hope was swiftly slipping away like a castle of sand being swept into the deep by the sea's waves. Could she manage to survive? Would there be the faintest glimmer of hope in her dark world?

If only she could do something to make herself more loveable. It seemed to be the feelings of confusion that created the most depression and sense of hopelessness. She had lived with depression, confusion, and disconnectedness from self most of her life, and had learned to cope, but now these seemed to be worsening.

Prisoner was just about to the end of her rope when she remembered her water jar. Surely, there was something in the water jar to meet her desperate need. She found the water jar and clutched it tightly like a frightened child clinging to a rag doll for comfort. By this time in Prisoner's life, the water jar was bulging from the enormous amount of trash she had stuffed into it.

Digging deeply into the water jar, she pulled out something from her past that just might work. *While*

*I was in High School, and after I had been molested
and suffered much humiliation, I became very loose,
morally. I hated myself for the way I had lived then—
the many sins in my life. However, for a short time
I felt I was loved—that I was wanted—that I had a
small amount of significance. If it worked then, it
should work now; besides, I'm desperate—without
the feeling I have some value, I will surely die!* With
these kinds of thoughts motivating her behavior,
she bathed herself, painted her face with the small
amount of makeup she had gotten enough money to
buy, and went out for a night on the town.

Prisoner decided to spend her nights searching
for love in a neighboring town. She hoped there
would be no gossip if she went to a town where
she was unknown to the vast majority. Every night,
she prowled the streets like a cat in heat, but every
Sabbath she was faithful to attend the worship at the
temple on Mt. Gerizim.

Perhaps, *chameleon* best describes what Prisoner
had become because she was constantly changing,
blending in with whatever her surroundings were
at any given moment. In the temple, she seemed so
innocent, almost angelic as she worked harder than
ever to gain acceptance of God and people. However,
when walking the streets at night, she was anything
except angelic.

Prisoner had become the master of deception,
piling lie upon lie every time anyone from Sychar
asked her where she went at night. She used every
excuse she could think of to explain her where-
abouts—everything from visiting a sick friend to

working another part-time job. *Why can't people just mind their own business? Can they not understand how desperate I am?* Prisoner thought. She was growing weary of attempting to explain everything to everyone. In actuality, she was running out of excuses; she wondered how long she would be able to keep up this charade.

One night, as she made her routine excursion to the nearby town, Prisoner decided to stop at a bar. She had heard there were numerous single, eligible, young bachelors who frequented the bar. *Who knows,* she thought, *maybe tonight will be my lucky night.*

Prisoner sat down at the bar beside a very handsome hunk-of-a-man. His wavy, dark hair and piercing, hazel-green eyes enhanced the strikingly sharply chiseled features of his face. She could not help but notice his bulging muscles and thought about the many hours he must spend at the gym. Immediately she thought, *I don't know about this guy. I need someone who will always be there for me, not someone who is going to spend most of his time off from work in the gym. Maybe I should not give him a second thought.*

As Prisoner positioned herself on the barstool, debating whether she should order a drink or not, her eyes met his. Her heart melted from the heat of his gaze. He introduced himself and asked what her name was and where she was from, etcetera. Smalltalk— for this Prisoner was thankful, as she had never been able to develop social skills that allowed her to bare her heart and soul to anyone.

This good-looking man asked Prisoner if he could buy her a drink. "No thank you," she replied. "Not a social drinker, huh," the man said with a slight chuckle. "Oh well, you can't say I didn't offer." Prisoner became afraid he would lose interest in her; she also thought he was laughing at her and felt somewhat intimidated. Turning back to make eye contact, she said, "I suppose a little wine wouldn't hurt anything."

Prisoner had always felt it was wrong to drink alcoholic beverages, although she could not say why she believed this. She had never known the affliction of growing up in the home of an alcoholic parent, as some of her friends had; however, when Prisoner was very young, her father would drink beer and occasionally come home *stewed to the gills*. Perhaps these few painful episodes of seeing her father drunk were the tools that engraved in her the belief that drinking was wrong.

The time had come for Prisoner to put away these childish beliefs concerning right and wrong. She had a desperate need, and she was willing to do almost anything to have that need satisfied. As she squelched the voice within that was telling her she was headed for trouble, she put the glass of wine to her lips not knowing what to expect as the warm, smooth drink rolled over her tongue and down her throat.

Prisoner finished the glass of wine, and the man she had just met ordered another drink for her. She was beginning to like the taste of the wine, but she enjoyed more the way it made her feel. For someone who was so cold and desolate of soul, the wine delivered a soothing flow of warmth. Inhibitions disappeared, and for the first time in her life, Prisoner was able to carry on a conversation with someone without fear of saying the wrong thing or being misunderstood.

The morning sun rose in a brilliant display of color over the top of the mountain that shadowed the city. Hues of blue, gray, pink, purple, red, and orange led the parade introducing the sun that glistened like a gigantic golden ball in the sky. Anyone would have gladly awakened with the first hint of morning light to view such a radiant show; however, it would be several more hours before Prisoner could manage to rid herself of the wine's effect enough to raise her heavy eyelids.

The sun had made its way high in the middle of the sky before Prisoner began to stir from her sleep. Her head throbbed with pain that was indescribable, and she felt as though she could feel each beat of her pulse inside her head. Prisoner did not know where she was or how she got there.

"How much wine did I drink last night?" Prisoner asked herself. She had no way of knowing exactly what had happened. She only knew she felt as though she had been beaten. Struggling to sit upright, she reached to brush her hair away from her face when she noticed a wedding band on her left hand. Through the dense fog, which enshrouded her mind, she attempted to figure out exactly where she was and what had happened when she realized she had acquired more than a wedding band from her one-night stand. It was no wonder she felt as though she

had been beaten—she had bruises and lacerations over her entire body, including two black, swollen eyes.

Prisoner began to look around and try to get oriented to her surroundings. She made her way to the kitchen of this dingy, dirty apartment, pulled an ice tray from the tiny freezer compartment, wrapped some ice in a dirty dishtowel she found laying on the counter, and held the ice on her eyes in hopes of relieving the excruciating pain.

Where was the man Prisoner had been with last night? *This must be his apartment,* she thought. *But where was he now? Oh, he must have gone to get medical help for me,* she tried to convince herself. The reality of what had happened the night before was beginning to creep across her memory, but any glimpses of truth Prisoner kept locked deep inside. She would not allow herself to think about the truth. Instead, she attempted to reassure herself the man she had spent the night with would come back and give her the love she so desperately needed.

Prisoner would have cried a river of tears had it not been for her unbearable pain, although she was so destitute of emotion she had no more tears left to cry. *"I must keep my wits about me; there are some major decisions to be made,"* she said to herself. Prisoner picked up a broom that was leaned against a corner in the kitchen with the good intention to begin cleaning this roach-infested apartment. Her pain and exhaustion would not allow her to follow through with her intention to clean, so she opted for the little bit of relief the lumpy, sagging mattress of the iron-framed bed could offer.

The beautiful sunshine of the day had fled, giving into the moonless, but star-studded sky, by the time Prisoner awoke from her deep sleep. She sat on the side of the bed waiting for her vision to adjust to the darkness and then stood up, fumbling for the light switch. Unable to dispel the darkness in the bedroom, she made her way to the tiny kitchen and turned on the light.

Prisoner had gotten over her nausea and was feeling very hungry, so she searched the refrigerator and cabinets for something to eat. All she could find were some stale crackers and dried-up, hard cheese. It was not very appetizing, but it was edible and sufficient to ease the gnawing hunger pains in her stomach.

Suddenly the reality of her predicament shot through her emotions like a carefully aimed arrow from the bow of The Archer of Heartbreak Alley. Prisoner was in an apartment somewhere in the heart of a city she barely knew anything about. Judging from the wedding band that was on her left hand, she was married to a man whom she had met only the night before—she was not even sure what the man's last name was. The most heart-wrenching truth of all was that Prisoner had again fallen prey to a man who did not fulfill her need for love. Not knowing when or if her new husband would return, Prisoner decided it was best to not eat any more right now, but rather to save the remainder of food and make it last until she could somehow manage to get more.

The next day, Prisoner scavenged her purse for her sunglasses. Although the weather was partly cloudy and she did not really need the sunglasses, she could not go out to look for a job while sporting those two black eyes of hers. Upon locating the sunglasses, which she hoped would divert attention away from her black eyes, she hurried out through the front door, determined to find a job.

The first two places Prisoner went to in search of employment were total washouts. Because she was uncertain of her husband's last name, and because she wished to keep her true identity a secret, she had decided beforehand to give a false name. She gave a name that sounded much like her real name so, hopefully, no one would become suspicious; however, everyone kept asking why she insisted on wearing the sunglasses when, by this time, the sky was almost completely overcast—and why did she continue to wear them while inside the buildings. She had learned to lie many years before when trying to escape the pain of her miserable life, so she always managed to come up with some excuse when asked the reason for the sunglasses.

The third place in which she sought employment proved fruitful, although she not only lied about the sunglasses but also, lied about her marital status as well. As she began filling out the application, Prisoner noticed that the employer preferred women employees to be single, so she quickly rationalized that it would be acceptable to say that she was not married: *After all, I do not know for certain that I'm married. The man has not been seen for several days.*

Perhaps, he just gave the ring to me out of friendship and there is no binding, legal document stating that we were married.

Very quickly, a month had passed, and Prisoner had managed to make enough money to clean and fix-up the apartment. Her black eyes had turned to purple, then blue, and then greenish yellow as she was finally able to shed her sunglasses. One morning, Prisoner was running a little late, so she decided to leave the bed unmade, and as she emptied her coffee cup of the last sip of coffee, she placed the cup in the sink and dashed off to work.

That evening when Prisoner was finished with work for another day, she boarded the bus for the apartment that had come to be her home for the past month. As the bus's wheels grinded to a halt at the bus stop, Prisoner got off and began her one-block trek to the apartment, but she had no way of knowing what awaited her there. When she was a few yards from the apartment, she noticed a car parked there, which she had never seen before.

Placing her right hand on the doorknob to open the door, she was frightened half out of her wits as the doorknob jerked from her grasp and the door flew open. There she stood with mouth dropped open in confusion and fright, face-to-face, nose-to-nose and eye-to-eye with a man. In the split second of silence that followed, she recognized him as the man she had met in the bar—the man to whom she was evidently married.

He grasped Prisoner's long, dark hair and jerked her inside the door. "Where have you been?" the man yelled. "And what do you think you're doing?"

"I might ask you the same questions," Prisoner replied. "Don't you like the way I've fixed-up the apartment?" she asked in a trembling voice, in hopes of pleasing him.

"Fixed-up the apartment!" He yelled so loud that Prisoner's ears rang with pain. "What do you mean? I placed a wedding band on your finger because you wanted to get married even though the last thing I wanted was to be tied down with a wife to care for! I left you in this nice apartment, and I come home to find you haven't been taking care of the place. Look at it! The bed is not made—you left dirty dishes in the sink. Now, what do you think—should I reward you for such childish behavior?"

"I didn't know you were coming back—or if you were coming back," Prisoner began to sob. For an entire month, she had been unable to cry; why did she have to start crying now? She sensed that her crying would only agitate her husband, so she tried to hold back the tears but was unable to stop the flow that etched its way through her makeup and down her cheeks.

"Stop your bawling! You're nothing but a baby, so I guess I'd better teach you a lesson!" He began slapping Prisoner in the face and shoving her from one room to another as she tripped over furniture and tried to shield herself from his horrific blows.

"Why don't you just leave?" she cried.

"Leave," he laughed. "Aren't you forgetting this is my apartment?"

"Then I'll leave," she sobbed, and she headed for the bedroom to get her clothes.

He grabbed her arm and spun her around, almost pulling her arm from its socket. "You're not going anywhere sweetie! You're my wife and you will do as I say. Understand?"

"Yes, I understand, but what about my job?" she asked.

"Oh, you'll have to quit. No wife of mine is going to work at a place where there are men working. Besides, I won't have people saying I can't provide for my wife," he said with a wicked sneer on his face.

That wicked sneer sent a chill up Prisoner's spine as her memory raced back many years to the time her molester had threatened her, and then glared at her with the same sort of wickedly convincing sneer. She was very frightened and spent most of the night in the corner, crouched in a fetal position, and praying that God would intervene.

She arose with the first light of morning in hopes this man, who had once melted her heart with his tender eyes but who now seemed to have a heart of stone, was gone away from the apartment. No such luck—He was still there and wanted to know why she had gotten up so early. "Well, I have to fix our breakfast and then find a phone so I can call and tell them I will not be working anymore," she explained.

"No, you won't phone-in your resignation; you will go down there in person and resign. You need to tell them you have decided to stay home because your husband wants you at home. Understand?"

"Yes," she reluctantly replied.

"Well, you're a fast learner," he derided. "By the way, I need to make a correction to your previous statement. You *want* to fix breakfast; it's something you want to do, and not something you *have* to do. Again, you will fix *my* breakfast, and not *our* breakfast."

Prisoner knew she must not cross this man, or she would again be suffering the pain of black eyes. She began scurrying around to fix his breakfast, get dressed, and make it to the bus stop on time. He asked her why she was in such a hurry. She explained that she had to make it to the bus stop in time to catch the bus. He said, "You won't be riding the bus; that's money you can save for me." In protest, she explained it was several miles to where she had worked, and she could never make it that far. He only laughed and suggested that maybe some guy would stop and give her a lift; then he would have an excuse for beating them both.

Prisoner went into the bedroom, put on her coat, and reached for her purse. She had managed to cram a few clothes underneath her coat and into her purse, along with her toothbrush and a comb. It was her intention to get as far away from that apartment, that man, and that town as possible. Trying to think of a way out of the house without his noticing she had taken some of her belongings, she was startled half out of her wits when the bedroom door flung open and the man yelled angrily that Prisoner had best get on her way.

She stood frozen, eyes wide and staring at this man who claimed to be her husband. "Well, what are you waiting for?" he yelled. As his words rang in her ears, Prisoner was able to move from her frozen stance. Immediately clutching her coat tightly around her and praying the clothes she had stuffed under her coat would not fall out to the floor and that the clothes would not be noticed, she hurried past the man and out the front door.

Prisoner half walked, half ran down the street until she was out of sight of the apartment. Thoughts raced through her head as she tried to decide what to do first and where to go. She was headed for her place of employment when she stopped suddenly in her tracks. *I can't go in there and tell them I will no longer be working for them!* she thought. *This will raise too many questions. It will be too humiliating to try to explain, especially since I had to say I was not married in order to get the job!*

Running as fast as she could past the place she had worked, she made her way to the southeast side of town—the road leading to Sychar, her hometown. Prisoner paused to catch her breath and thought, *I have no other choice; I must go home!* She fumbled through her purse for some money to pay for a phone call and rushed to the nearest phone. Gulping down her pride as well as her tears, she hurriedly dialed the number of her parents' house. *"Oh, please be there,"* she whispered.

After numerous rings, her mom finally answered the phone. Prisoner briefly explained where she was and asked if her mom or dad would come and pick her up. Her mom began asking many questions about where Prisoner had been and what was happening. "Please, mom, I don't have time to explain now!" Prisoner pleaded. Her mother told Prisoner that both she and her dad would leave as soon as she hung up the phone. Then Prisoner added, "I'm going to start walking, so you will find me on the road. Please hurry!" She hung up the phone and ran as fast as she could toward Sychar, looking back over her shoulder from time to time for fear her husband had followed her.

By the time her parents found her along the road, Prisoner was completely exhausted and somewhat dehydrated. Her dad stopped the car and Prisoner stumbled into the back seat and laid there gasping for breath. Naturally, her mother and father wanted to question her but realized she was too tired to answer any questions at this time.

The trip back to Sychar, which only took about ten minutes, seemed to take forever. Finally home, her parents helped Prisoner into the house, gave her some fruit juice to drink, and then helped her to the bedroom. Her old bedroom had not been changed in any way since she had left home the first time. There would be time for reminiscing later—right now, she needed rest.

Prisoner slept for two days, only waking occasionally to drink some water and/or fruit juice and go to the bathroom. In the meantime, her parents were becoming very anxious to receive some answers to their many questions. When she finally began to wake up enough to realize where she was, she knew she must answer truthfully her parents' questions.

Although she was somewhat disoriented as she began to stir from her slumber, she did her best to explain and to answer the many questions her parents posed. She lived in constant fear throughout the months that followed—fear her husband would find her and take her back only to be beaten and humiliated for the rest of her life.

Once again, she became faithful to attend the services at the church on Mt. Gerizim in hopes she could forget her past, find peace of mind, and get on with her life. However, as the questions and whisperings increased, she found every excuse to stay away from the church and away from the center of town.

Prisoner had been back in her parents' home for almost a year. In many ways, it seemed she had been back home for only a short time, but in other ways, it seemed as though she had never left. Although she found it quite depressing each time she walked in her old bedroom, she realized the room was a lot like her—nothing had really changed. The furniture and décor had gotten older and so had she. Gently running her fingers over the lace curtains that framed the window, her mind went back to the many times she had cried herself to sleep, longing for someone to love her and take her away from all the pain.

A firm knock on the front door jolted Prisoner from her past memories and to the reality of the present. She peeked through the eyehole in the door to identify the person on the other side of the door. Never again would she open a door without first checking to see who was on the other side.

The young man at the door was wearing a uniform and held a letter, a notepad of sorts, and a pen in his hand. Prisoner recognized him as a postal worker and quickly opened the door. He presented her with a registered letter. She nervously signed for the letter and tore through the envelope, anxious to read the letter's contents, but also afraid of what words were written on the page.

As she read the contents, she began to sob, almost uncontrollably. Her husband, whom she had not heard from in nearly a year, had located her and sent the letter. Prisoner was ecstatic with joy because her husband was not coming to take her back, but instead was asking for a divorce. At last, she would finally be rid of him forever. Suddenly, her tears of joy became tears of confusion as she realized she was just as destitute as ever. Sure, her parents had been wonderful for allowing her to come back home, but she could not stay in their home forever. Prisoner must continue to search for love and significance — needs that, even through all of their kindnesses, her parents could not satisfy.

~~~~~~~~~~~~~~~

Wow! What a mess Prisoner has gotten herself into! Of course, many of you may be saying that this is the most absurd thing you have ever read and there is no way the woman at the well could have lived this kind of life. Allow me to remind you that Jesus did not go to the woman at the well in order to point out the fact that she was a Samaritan, but rather to confront her with the issue of her sin. Jesus went to Jacob's well for the explicit purpose of making this woman aware of her **true** need. For years, she had tried to satisfy her need for love, but Jesus showed her that she needed a Savior, not another human relationship.

I would like to pose some questions to you: How did it happen that this woman had been married five times before her encounter with Jesus, and at the time of His meeting her, she was living with a man to whom she was not married? Is it possible the events in her life could have developed in ways similar to what I have written? Have you ever known someone who bears a shocking similitude to this woman—running to relationship after relationship? Do you recognize yourself and the events of your life (present or past), even so slightly, analogous to this saga?

If you are honest, no doubt you would have answered yes to all of the above questions, with the exception of the first question. Now, back to question number one—why did the woman at the well marry and divorce five times? Except for the grace of God, her story could belong to any one of us! When we pause and carefully ponder the "whys" concerning the direction this woman's life took, this story does not seem to be so far-fetched after all.

I confess right now! Much of Prisoner's life bears a marked resemblance to my own. Although I have only been married to one man, and vowed that one time to be married was enough, I have had many difficulties with relationships through the years. For the largest portion of my life, I was extremely depressed, I had difficulty making friends, and I desperately needed to know I mattered to someone.

My family was extremely performance driven; therefore, I thought happiness, significance, and any similitude of normalcy could be achieved only if I performed well enough. Frankly, I always felt as though I could never measure up to anyone's expectations, though I exhausted myself in the attempt to do so. Pleasing everyone and trying to meet their expectations of what defines who we are is an impossible task because to please everyone is not the reason God gives us life and places us on this Earth.

Life would have been much more peaceful and enjoyable if I had left my water jar with Jesus and looked to Him, the Living Water, to satisfy every need of my heart. However, I continued to walk in the wilderness for many years. There were some spurts of spiritual growth, some moments when I felt God's presence and knew I was in His will, but these moments were too few, and too much distance lay between these moments to engender any lasting, deeply rooted, spiritual benefit.

Yes, I had made it out of Egypt, but the trip through the wilderness was indescribable because the wilderness is a desolate place of misguided direction. I use the term, *misguided direction,* because when you are so destitute and are trying to find a way to have those needs met, you constantly search for satisfaction in sort of a trial-and-error fashion. You look in one direction and think to yourself, *This way looks like it might be the right way out of this wilderness. Perhaps if I go this way, I will have my needs met.* Therefore, we continue to go ways that appear to us to be the right ways, but in actuality, we are misguided and continue to go the wrong direction. Just like the Israelites, I made numerous trips around Mount Sinai in a constant struggle to *get my act together*, but instead I continued to wander around in circles—going nowhere except farther away from the security of my Heavenly Father and the love He was longing to lavish on me.

In addition, the wilderness is a dry place, and I can testify that there is no *dry* like spiritually dry. I had experienced salvation; I had the Living Water inside of me, but still I was dry because I chose to remain in the wilderness rather than drinking daily from the fountain of Living Water.

Now, what about you my friend, my brother, my sister—where are you in your journey? Are you living in destitution, very needy, and yet you feel there is no hope of having those needs met? Are you lugging that heavy water jar through the wilderness thinking it holds the solution for your problems, as you search endlessly for love and significance?

God allows us to enter the wilderness for a purpose. Because our Heavenly Father loves us so much, He allows wilderness experiences in order that we may learn to trust Him implicitly and come to know that He is our all in all. In other words, like the Prodigal (Luke 15:17a), we must become destitute enough that we finally come to our senses and realize, "I cannot meet my needs, neither can any other human being completely bring satisfaction, so I will go to the One who can—my Heavenly Father."

There is a way out of the wilderness, but it is impossible for us to find the way out if we only rely on our own strength and power. Until we realize and admit how destitute we are, we will continue to wander aimlessly in the wilderness. Pride convinces us we are capable in our own strength to meet our needs. No doubt, we all agree pride is sin. This sin of pride causes us to be continually misguided and prevents our finding the right way out of the wilderness of destitution. Therefore, we must confess we have sinned and ask God to forgive us. Do not remain destitute, for spiritual destitution is only one step above spiritual destruction. Instead, cry out to God—"I call on You in the day of my distress, for You will answer me" (Psalm 86:7, HCSB)—and look to Him alone to satisfy your every need—"They ate and were completely satisfied, for He gave them what they craved" (Psalm 78:29, HCSB).

CHAPTER FIVE

Destroyed

We have examined the first three strategies that Satan uses to keep the lost in their present state, separated from God, and to prevent born-again believers from having God's best. Now, it is time to take an up-close look at the last and final step at the bottom of this winding staircase, which leads to the pit.

The fourth and final strategy the Enemy makes use of in bringing about his agenda is to destroy us. What does it mean to be destroyed? Let's take a look at the meaning as is found in the *Webster's New Dictionary of the English Language*:

- **destroy** *vb* **1:** to put an end to**:** RUIN **2:** KILL

The Devil, Satan, the Destroyer, the Enemy is set on one thing—destroying us. It was his desire to destroy the woman at the well. He wanted to put an end to any hopes she might have for a good life and any possibility of her being saved. He wanted to so ruin her that she would not be able to hear the voice of God inviting her to know salvation. Finally, he wanted to kill her—spiritually, emotionally, and physically.

Satan is in no hurry to destroy us—he is simply tenacious in his efforts of determined destruction. Because he is very patient and persistent in his efforts, he brings us down one step at a time by using these four strategies: to desensitize us, to demoralize us, to make us destitute, and to destroy us. Satan does not usually barge right into our lives, but instead he gains entrance little by little. As far back in history as the Garden of Eden, we can see how the Enemy has employed these strategies, so I have no reason to believe his dealings with the woman at the well were any different—I know he used these four strategies in my life. Unfortunately, I endured a stint in each of these four strategies before I finally wised-up, cried out to God in repentance, and began to develop an intimate relationship with Him.

As we continue with the story of Prisoner, try to recall from the previous chapters that the road to destruction is sometimes a very long road. In other words, she did not become stagnated in malfunction overnight. She did not go to bed one night, a happy, vibrant, well-adjusted young lady and wake up the next morning depressed, filled with fear, feeling unloved and utterly hopeless. No, it was a gradual process, spanning many years, which brought her to the point of destruction. With that said, we will return to the story and find out what Prisoner will do next.

~~~~~~~~~~~~~~~

Prisoner went to her room, fell across the bed, and cried until there were no more tears left to cry. She was happy her husband, whom she hardly knew, was stepping out of her life for good, but at the same time, she felt overwhelmed by a sense of guilt, shame, anger, and fear. The feelings of guilt were the result of her immoral lifestyle; the shame resulted from feelings that something was wrong with her and therefore would never know love; the many years of stuffing the garbage into her water jar resulted in anger; her confusion over what to do next and where to go from here, resulted in fear.

Remembering the difficulty she had as a child understanding and coping with her emotions, she realized that, although she was older, she had not grown any wiser in this area of her life. When her mother and father would come to the door of her bedroom to inquire if she was okay, all she could say was she needed some time to think through some things. The shame and its many tentacles that continued for so many years to wrap around her soul and wind their way through the core of her being, caused her to be completely incapable of making the contradistinction between truth and lies—reality and fantasy.

Prisoner—still the sad one—still the quiet one—still the mistrusting one! For many years, she had tried to choose her words carefully in order to avoid humiliation and hurt. However, in her attempt to choose her words carefully, she could find nothing to say, and this only added to the frustration and depression of her emotional tug-of-war. Her parents were hurt to see her in such turmoil, but they could not find the right words, although they knew she needed to open up and talk about the issues at hand.

Well, the divorce was finalized at last, and Prisoner was a *free* woman! She was feeling a little better and decided it was time for her to go out more and to find a job—she even felt the need to go back to church. Prisoner also wanted to be out on her own and although her parents had said she could stay with them for as long as she wanted, Prisoner knew it would not work for the best if she had to live with them for an extended period.

After a few weeks of searching, Prisoner landed a job at the garment factory in her hometown of Sychar. The pay was not that great, but at least it was close to home and, for now, she did not have to worry about paying rent. There was one major drawback to this job—the night shift was the only opening they had. Working during the daylight hours had been difficult enough, but the fatigue, caused from the many years of living with depression, made working the night shift almost unbearable. However, Prisoner dragged herself to work night after night and gave it her all, as little as her all was, because she wanted to be a good worker.

Prisoner put in long nighttime hours at the factory, but that did not prevent her attending worship on Mt. Gerizim. She still had much insecurity and felt like such a failure, so in her twisted way of thinking, she felt that if there was penance, if there was enough self-punishment, all of the garbage from her past would somehow be erased from the minds of the people in the pew. After all, she had changed; she had come home and vowed to be good.

Prisoner may have desired to do what was right, perhaps even changed somewhat for the good, but she fell into the same old trap of trying to prove to everyone that she was good. *I wonder what it feels like to not have to prove that you are worthy,* Prisoner thought. *Oh well, I messed up so badly it is only right that I must prove myself acceptable—that I have some worth.*

As Prisoner sat in her usual spot in the worship service and stared ahead at the preacher in the pulpit, her mind went back to a time in adolescence when she had worked so hard at the church in an attempt to feel some sense of significance. *I was only a child,* Prisoner thought, *but I did feel a certain amount of approval, love, and accomplishment.* As soon as she was confident the congregation had accepted her again, she began to volunteer for every job at the church, which came available.

One evening Prisoner went into the bathroom and started getting ready for work. As she looked into the hollow eyes that stared back at her in the mirror, she began telling herself what a worthless, horrible failure she was. Working the long nights at her job and trying to *perform* all of the tasks at the church was proving to be too much for her to bear. Unbidden tears began to flow down her cheeks as she admitted she was involved in too many activities.

Drying her tears and looking back into the mirror, she realized allergies were not the sole reason for the dark circles under her eyes. *I can't stop now,* she thought—*at least I must continue what I am doing at the church. People are just beginning to like me, accept me, and love me … but I cannot quit my job either. What I need is a husband—a real husband who will love me and provide for me.* With this last thought still ringing in her head, work for this partic- ular evening became secondary, and off she went to the factory on her manhunt.

As she arrived at work that evening, one of the male employees caught her eye. The man had grown up in Sychar and graduated from Sychar High School. Prisoner asked herself why she had not really noticed this man before. Perhaps she had not noticed him before now because he was almost ten years her senior; why, she was only a child when he was graduated from high school. However, she was now a woman, not a child, and the number of years that spanned their ages did not make that much difference, so Prisoner began to view this man as a prospective husband.

Prisoner sat near the man when they took one of the ten-minute breaks that evening. She sensed that he was somewhat shy, so, even though it was extremely difficult for her, she initiated the conver- sation. Before the ten minutes was over, he began to open up and talk to her. As they talked, some things he said made Prisoner realize her reputation had preceded her. She immediately became fearful that he would not think well of her, so she probed further in order to find out exactly how much this man knew about her past. Maybe he knew more about her than he let her know, but she was relieved that either he did not know all of her wicked past, or her past did not seem to bother him.

That week at work proved a profitable one for Prisoner because as the end of the week was approaching, the man asked her for a date. Luckily, neither she nor the man had to work that Saturday evening, so they made a date for dinner and a movie. "I'll pick you up at six o'clock," the man called to her as he headed for his car to go home. "That's great. I'll be ready," Prisoner replied.

Prisoner awoke earlier than usual on Saturday. Normally, she was so tired that she slept most of the day, but today was different. She was excited, hopeful, and yet, somewhat fearful concerning what the future might hold for her relationship with this man.

Prisoner told her mother and father about the man and assured them he was a gentleman. She reminded them the man had grown up in Sychar, had never married, and went to church regularly.

"But he is too old for you," Prisoner's mother protested.

"Age makes no difference," Prisoner replied, "besides, it's only a date; we're not planning marriage!"

"Does he know you have been married three times already," her mother questioned.

"I'm not sure," said Prisoner.

"Well, you need to tell him," her mother insisted.

"If I need to tell him, then I will," Prisoner snapped back.

"Why did he ask you out in the first place?" her mother asked. Prisoner looked surprised by the question. Her mother continued, "I mean why would a man ten years older than you want to go out with you—especially if he has any inkling of your escapades?" Prisoner remained silent.

Mother has not changed one iota! She still has no love in her heart for me, Prisoner thought as she held back the tears. *Why wouldn't he want to go out with me,* she questioned. Suddenly, Prisoner was so overwhelmed by shame she considered breaking the date. Her mother was sorry her words had not come out exactly as she had intended, but could not find the strength to say, "I'm sorry."

Prisoner went on the date and had an especially good time. They began spending more and more time together, and within a few months were considering marriage. So far, she had managed to avoid all conversation concerning her past, and she did not dare ask questions about his past. When he popped the question, she immediately said that she would be honored to be his wife, almost as if she wanted to reply before either of them changed their mind.

After sharing with her parents her plans for marriage, a million questions and thoughts flooded through Prisoner's mind. *What if he doesn't really love me? He is quite a few years older than I am—oh well, perhaps his age will add some stability to my life. Should I tell him everything about my past before we get married, or should I wait until we've been married a few years? Perhaps I should not tell him anything—my past is past, right?* Prisoner continued this seesaw of questioning and reasoning right until the time the "I do's" were said.

Prisoner and her fiancé had decided a large wedding was not for them. In fact, they decided that simply to stand before the mayor of Sychar to repeat their vows was all they wanted. At last, the day came when Prisoner found herself hooked to husband number four. The simple ceremony in the mayor's office was okay with Prisoner, but she did not like the idea of not going away somewhere for a honeymoon. However, she did not say anything about the disappointment of not having a honeymoon; instead, she tucked this disenchantment away in her water jar for *safekeeping*.

It was not many months after the consummation of this relationship before the **sweet** bliss of marriage began to boil, producing the ugliness of bitterly **sour** disharmony. Prisoner tried to please husband number four, at least in the beginning, but it looked as if she could do nothing to meet his expectations concerning the kind of wife she should be.

Prisoner and her husband disagreed and argued about things that did not really matter, such as, whether or not the toothpaste tube should be squeezed from the bottom of the tube or the middle of the tube. What made him think he had the right to complain about her cooking; after all, she had been practicing for a long time because she was just a child in elementary school when her mother had taught her to cook, sew, and care for a house. She viewed herself as a good cook, but her husband constantly complained about the meals she prepared saying, "It doesn't taste the same as it did when my mother prepared this particular dish."

In addition, Prisoner had never been frivolous in her spending of money, but her husband made a fuss any time she spent some money without consulting him first, especially if she bought something for herself. Therefore, Prisoner felt the pangs of intimidation because, from her perspective, her husband was treating her more as if she was his child rather than his wife. These disagreements about her management of the household funds were particularly painful for Prisoner. Like a huge, festered sore that gushes with pus when lanced, all of the old wounds from her past were reopened, spewing forth her feelings of inadequacy, insecurity, shame, anger, and fear, and she became more depressed, dysfunctional, and disconnected each time he scolded her for spending money.

Every disagreement they engaged in would eventually escalate into a shouting match. Both Prisoner and her husband fell into the trap of attempting to *pass the buck*; neither of them would admit any fault in their arguments. Communication between them was nil—good communication, that is. It had always been difficult for Prisoner to talk and share her feelings because she had learned a long time ago that no one is worthy of trust, so she resolved to be quiet and keep the peace at any cost.

In the midst of the many arguments, Prisoner and her husband determined to keep up their fairytale façade when in public. They continued to attend church every time the doors were open. Yes, when it came time to go to church, they put on their best smiles and their best demeanor and went to church. Because it was so important that everyone in town think highly of them, authenticity had almost become a dirty word. They each thought, *I can never allow anyone to know how we really are and what goes on in our home.*

Prisoner become more depressed and disconnected from her husband and herself with each passing day. However, with the tenacity of a bulldog, she continued to fulfill her obligations at the church on Mt. Gerizim and was as equally determined to become the kind of wife her husband wanted. Try as she did, her depression gave way to increased fatigue and the fatigue to increased depression, so she was simply too overwhelmed by her circumstances to continue in these nonsensical activities. She had been knocking herself out to please her husband, and he did not seem to care. The work she was involved in at church was proving to be more than she had bargained for also. It was much to her relief when her husband suggested the marriage was not working and they should divorce; she gladly conceded to his suggestion.

In the few weeks following the divorce, Prisoner tried to convince herself that her fourth husband was too old and too set in his ways to know how to love someone like her. She had become a very angry person over the years, but because she never had a propensity toward fits of rage, she did not perceive her feelings as anger. In particular, Prisoner was angry with her mother because she felt her mother had failed in preparing her for marriage and the real world. In stunned silence, Prisoner, for a few moments, was lost in her thoughts—thoughts of days gone by and thoughts concerning the "what ifs" of life: *My mother taught me how to cook, sew, and care for a house, but she failed to teach me how to care for a husband. If I could have been more like mother, perhaps I would still be married to my first husband—although, I'm not so certain women are to wait on their husbands hand-and-foot as she did for my father. She idolized my father—idolatry is sin. I cannot deny the fact that they seemed to have a good relationship, but there did not seem to be any room or love for me. If my mother and father had loved me, then I would have known how to give love and receive love. Where was my place of refuge and security when I was molested—when I felt the pain of shame, rejection, and intimidation?*

It did not take Prisoner long to rebound from her pity party. After a few weeks of rest, she was able to once again stuff all of her unpleasant memories into her water jar. One day, she was talking to one of the ladies from the church on Mt. Gerizim. The lady said, "Prisoner, I've been thinking about you and your happiness. Please, allow me to give you some advice. The anecdote for your plight is a good man."

"I don't know about that," Prisoner responded.

"When something doesn't go as it should, you must try again. It's like when you fall off a horse—you get up and get right back on the horse again," the lady chided. "Believe me—what you need is another relationship to fill the void left by your ex-husband. Love is what you need."

"I know I need love," Prisoner said with a hint of desperation in her voice. "But where am I going to find another husband—a husband who will love me unconditionally, considering what I have been through?"

"I know just the man for you—he's my brother," the lady anxiously replied. "He's been married before also, so he can understand your situation and your feelings."

"I have not been divorced very long—don't you think it may be a little too soon to think about marrying again?" Prisoner questioned.

"Just go out with him a few times; if you don't like each other, you don't need to get married. However, I wouldn't wait too long if I were you; you're not getting any younger, you know," the lady said in an intimidating manner.

Prisoner decided this lady was right and that she should try right away to find someone else to love her. Besides, she really did not want to reenter the workforce, so finding the right man would be an *easy out* for her. The first date with the lady's brother left Prisoner in a very hopeful state. He was the kindest man, the gentlest man, and yet, the strongest man she had ever met. Prisoner thought this was surely *love-at-first-sight*. He seemed to truly care about her feelings, so when he proposed marriage a few months later, she gladly accepted, thinking that at last she had found a man who knew what love is all about. Although she found it easy to talk to him, there were some things from her past that were tightly sealed and that she would talk to no one about. As a result, she brought to the relationship all of the unresolved, unhealthy contents of her enormously large water jar.

Well, Prisoner is ready to enter into her fifth nuptial contract, and for some reason, she just feels this time the marriage is going to last a lifetime. Unfortunately, the feeling that she had found the perfect man began to slowly trickle into the black hole of her own struggle to know who she was. Her husband was a good man, a loving man who provided well for her, yet at the same time, he was extremely controlling. Prisoner felt bound by his insistence that she go nowhere without him, not even to the grocery store.

Perhaps his attempts to control her every move was the reason for her frustration and disconnectedness. Whatever the cause, Prisoner, more often than not, found herself standing in the shadows and viewing herself from afar. *I must find myself,* Prisoner thought. *I simply cannot go on like this any longer.* Grasping for some inclination of the girl she was and the woman she was meant to be, *desperation* clutched his bony fingers around her neck, almost chocking the life out of her. Uncertain of what to do, she made the same choice she had made before—to call it quits.

Now that she was divorced again, Prisoner knew it was imperative for her to go back to work. Her parents were in poor health, and not wanting to impose upon them, she found an apartment near her work. *I suppose this is my destiny, my fate,* Prisoner reasoned within herself. *One thing is for sure—I will never marry again. In fact, I am beginning to believe the need for love and significance are not true needs, only desires. I do not need anyone!*

Often, Prisoner's parents asked her to drop by and see them. She obliged them even though she always felt like a stranger in their home. There seemed to always be an uneasiness and unwelcoming feeling, as though she was an intruder, and usually the visits ended in an argument with words being spoken that everyone later regretted.

Early one morning, around 5:30 AM, Prisoner received a call from one of her sisters. The call was to inform her that their father had died in his sleep. Prisoner hurriedly dressed and rushed to her parents' home where she and her siblings began making funeral arrangements. She wanted to grieve because she had heard that it was healthy to grieve in the right way, but the tears would not flow, neither was there any manifestation of anger or hurt. She appeared to be cold and insensitive to others attending the funeral, but the fact is, she was empty—she had nothing to give. So thick and so high was the wall she had built around her heart that words of comfort and encouragement could not find even the tiniest crevice by which to enter.

A few weeks after her father's funeral, she began to notice people around town were doing a lot of whispering as she walked down the street. *I suppose my past mistakes and failures have finally caught up with me,* Prisoner thought. *Who needs these gossipers, anyway? Friendship is a nice commodity but not a necessity!*

To work in the morning and back home in the evening—this is what Prisoner's day consisted of. She became more and more of a recluse, only leaving the house to go to work and to the grocery store. Her depression was worsening, if it was possible for it to grow worse, and she spent every moment while at home, asleep. She began to have severe headaches that prevented her from adequately performing her job, and when the headaches became more frequent and more severe, Prisoner decided to see a doctor.

After the doctor examined Prisoner and asked, what seemed to her to be, a million unnecessary questions, he prescribed Fiorinol™, which contained a barbiturate, to help her rest at night. That evening after seeing the doctor, she took the first dose of medicine, and within thirty to forty-five minutes, she had drifted off into a deep sleep. *Wow, I don't think I have slept so peacefully and for that many hours at one time since I was a baby,* Prisoner thought. *It certainly felt good to get some rest for a change.*

The one drawback to her night of peaceful rest was the medicine made her so sleepy that she had a difficult time functioning at work. She increased her intake of caffeine in an effort to be alert enough to do her job, but nothing seemed to help. However, Prisoner did not want to become so alert that the medicine failed to produce the sense of utopia she had come to enjoy every night. At least, she felt no emotional pain when the medicine was in control.

Nothing about Prisoner's life had changed over the years, unless it had changed for the worse and not the better. Whenever she went to the marketplace of Sychar or to the well that stood in the middle of the town square, she noticed that people shunned her more than ever before, especially the women did. Their obvious dispersion the moment she approached them was easily detected, and to Prisoner, their whispering behind her back sounded more like a trumpet than whispers—a trumpet heralding every shameful, disgusting thing about her life.

She heard the names they called her, names that triggered the memory of being molested and the name her perpetrator had called her. It hurt to know what others thought about her. One name they called her she felt could not be denied, *Trash*. She felt like trash! Her view of self, others, and the world in which she lived had become more distorted than a funhouse mirror. Everything about her was out of kilter and she had had enough. *"I simply cannot go on any further,"* she whispered aloud to herself. *"Something must be done to squelch this aching in my heart."*

Instead of taking her medicine at bedtime as she normally did, she took one pill immediately after dinner. Then she waited a couple of hours then took another pill. After taking only two pills, she was fast asleep. Very early the next morning the faithful alarm clock began its beckoning call for Prisoner to wake up, and upon arising, she took another pill. She dispensed with breakfast, and approximately thirty to forty-five minutes after taking the first pill, she took another one.

At work that day, Prisoner continued popping a pill about every fifteen to twenty minutes throughout most of the day. Just before quitting time, she felt as though she could not keep her eyes open and went into an unused storage room to rest for a while. Once inside the room, she sank to the floor, closed her eyes, and thought, *Is this the end for me? Am I about to go to sleep to never wake up again?* She fell asleep for what seemed to be a very long time, but in actuality, she was only asleep for approximately twenty minutes.

Suddenly, she felt someone's hand fall firmly on her shoulder, and begin to determinedly shake her, arousing her from her slumber. She jumped and looked around to see absolutely no one, only a tightly closed door. Managing to pull herself up from the floor, she opened the door, and stumbled into a coworker who *just happened* to be walking down the hall at this time. The coworker called for help and they rushed Prisoner to the emergency room of a nearby hospital.

Inside the emergency room, the doctor immediately began a gastric lavage. The gurney that Prisoner was laying on felt more like a marble slab, and her back began to hurt, but the back pain did not take her mind off the discomfort of having to swallow the lavage tube. Once her stomach had been cleansed of its contents, the doctor ordered a caffeine drip, 1,000 cc, of strong, black coffee to be administered rectally.

As Prisoner lay there in that emergency room, she desperately wanted to cry out and tell someone what she was feeling, and at the same time, she did not want to talk to anyone. She opted for the latter and kept her feelings to herself, tightly sealed in her water jar. The doctor probed to discover why she had taken the pills: "Prisoner, why did you do it? Why did you take all those pills? Did you want to die?" She could not muster the strength to answer, besides, she, herself, was not exactly sure why she had done it.

Her life lay in utter shambles! She knew that even though she was still alive, she was destroyed. Her reputation was ruined—all of her good deeds she had so faithfully performed on Mt. Gerizim would now have evil spoken of them. Yes, she was physically alive, but she had no real identity or purpose. She was like an empty shell, which had somehow sprouted feet and walked around. Both emotionally and spiritually, she had been killed—DESTROYED!

~~~~~~~~~~~~~~

It seems to be obvious that by the time she met Jesus, the woman at the well was destroyed, at least emotionally and spiritually. She, like we are so many times, was constantly grasping for something or someone to give meaning to her life. She was always taking action, trying to make things work on her own, without stopping to consider the possible consequences those actions would incur.

Prisoner, for whatever reasons, was caught in the vicious cycle of trying harder, things getting better for a while, and then experiencing a failure that was worse than the preceding failure. Instead of trusting God to satisfy her needs, she looked to others for love and acceptance. This lack of trust in God kept her bound in the destructive behaviors of running from one relationship to another. As the Psalmist said, "Here is the man who would not make God his refuge, but trusted in the abundance of his riches, taking refuge in his destructive behaviors" (Psalm 52:7, HCSB). I have observed this to be true in the lives of many women and men alike. They feel the solution to their relational difficulties is always to be found in another relationship.

The reason so many people run from bad marriage to bad marriage, is that none of their past issues are ever dealt with. How many times have you heard someone say to a person who is divorced, "You need to find a good man (or woman) to marry?" I heard my mother say some similar things as this to my oldest sister after her divorce. God may want that person to get married again at some point, but to rush into another relationship so that person will not be lonely or so they can know love and significance is not the answer to one's plight. No, the only relationship one should seek is a relationship with Jesus Christ.

I can completely relate to Prisoner's having been destroyed. By the time I was thirteen years of age,

I was so depressed I thought I was losing my mind. High school, which should have been one of the best times of my life, was one of the worst. Although I trusted Christ as my Savior when I was seven years old, the Enemy had destroyed me by the time I was eighteen. My destruction began with the ruining of my testimony before others. It only takes one poor choice that others are privy to for one's testimony to become tainted! Because I continued to make many wrong choices, I was rendered ineffective for the Kingdom's sake.

When I talked to Mrs. Gilbert, the counselor I referenced earlier in this book, about the depression and disconnectedness I experienced through most of my growing-up years, she was amazed at how I had covered it up and managed to function for as long as I did. I said to her, "If I had seen a psychologist or psychiatrist when I was at my worst, they probably would have diagnosed me as being schizophrenic, and I would have been in and out of the psychiatric ward, and placed on medication for the rest of my life." She agreed this is probably what would have transpired. Had that been the case, I would have never known the joy that an intimate relationship with Christ brings, and I would have never known the freedom of living in God's grace.

Due to certain unfortunate events in my life, the Enemy had robbed me of all joy and every good memory. I constantly hoped the contents of my water jar, things, which in times past had given me affirmation, would offer reassurance that I was loved and wanted—that I had some kind of worth and significance. Sure, I left my water jar with Jesus when I was seven years old, but I kept going back and picking it up again, lugging it around as if it were a trophy.

Yes, I was destroyed. Until a few short years ago, I could not remember even one solitary good thing about my life—growing up nor after I was married. I only remembered the wrong things I had done, the basketball games that were lost and I felt as though I was responsible, the times I had been hurt, the times I felt shame …, and the list went on.

I knew there were some accolades, such as receiving the Best Athlete Award two consecutive years, but somehow this memory had been twisted and distorted in my mind. I felt so undeserving and that there must be some ulterior motive for their giving me this award.

There was a filter comprised of my shortcomings that had been firmly glued to my mind preventing any good thing from passing through. Every victory, every accomplishment, every word of praise and/or encouragement was sifted through the sieve of all my inadequacies, insecurities, anxieties, and depression thereby keeping me enslaved and dwelling in the pit of destitution until I was finally destroyed.

Even after I was married, I tried to forget the painful memories of my past and create some good memories to be recalled in the near future, but to no avail. After about ten years into the marriage, I wanted to recall some pleasant memory, but I could only remember the times I had failed miserably. It became commonplace for me to remember the times I stood in church to sing a solo and had forgotten the lyrics, instead of the times when I sensed God's pleasure and people were touched by the message in song.

As our children made it through the difficult teenage years and into adulthood, I wanted to feel as though I had played a part for good in teaching them and shaping their character. However, I could only remember the times when I had made, what was in my perception, the wrong decision, and the times I had failed to properly teach them the ways of God, and the times I failed to show them how much I love them and how much their Heavenly Father loves them.

Then there were the years, for many and varied reasons, that I felt like a complete failure as a pastor's wife. Because of the depression, confusion, and fear, I was of no benefit to my pastor-husband or the church. Therefore, it is not difficult for me to understand that the woman at the well had been destroyed — emotionally, spiritually. It is also not difficult to understand that she had probably been destroyed for many years because she was looking in all the wrong places and trying in all the wrong ways to have her needs met.

Do you recall the wilderness I spoke of in the previous chapter? Allow me to refresh your memory: The wilderness is a place of misguided direction and a place of dryness. Lastly, the wilderness is a place of death and dying (Numbers 26:64-65).

When we, as believers in Christ, wander around in the wilderness, we will dehydrate from lack of Living Water. We begin to wither and waste away — dry up on the vine. A person who is physically dehydrated will often become confused and disoriented because of the imbalance in their electrolytes, and the same is true for the person who is spiritually dehydrated. The Enemy will put us to shame, confuse us, and strike fear in our hearts, thus causing us to die a slow agonizing spiritual death, rendering us useless in the Lord's service.

For the believer, Satan knows he can never have our soul—he cannot kill us and take us to hell. However, a Christian can choose to go so far away from God and His purpose for their life that they die prematurely. "If anyone sees his brother sinning a sin *which does* not *lead* to death, he will ask, and He will give him life for those who commit sin not *leading* to death. There is sin *leading* to death. I do not say that he should pray about that" (1John 5:16, NKJV).

In retrospect of my own life, I know the chastening hand of God continued to lay His scourge upon me for many years. I honestly believe I had gotten extremely close to committing the "sin unto death." Praise God for His mercy and compassion!

Dear brother and/or sister in Christ, even if you are lying on the floor of your pit, it is not too late—Jesus will lift you out of that pit! Reach out and take hold of His hand through true repentance. In the last strategy the Devil uses, as in the strategies prior, God is waiting for His penitent child to come home. If we repent, He will forgive: "[9]If we confess *our* sins, He is faithful and just to forgive us our sins and to cleanse us from all unrighteousness. [10]If we say that we have not sinned, we make Him a liar, and His word is not in us. [2:1]My little children, these things I write to you, so that you may not sin. And if anyone sins, we have an Advocate with the Father, Jesus Christ the righteous" (1John 1:9-2:1, NKJV).

If you have never received Christ as your Savior, come to Him now. You need a Savior, so if there is the slightest twinge of conviction, ask Him to forgive you and save you. Even if you feel as though you have been destroyed so much God would not have anything to do with you, He loves you and is willing to save you. Please, come to Jesus now before Satan completely destroys you and takes you to hell for eternity.

CHAPTER SIX

Delivered

As I look back over my life after salvation, it becomes clear Satan employed the four strategies of being desensitized, demoralized, destitute, and finally destroyed, in an attempt to prevent my having God's best and to prevent my fulfilling God's purpose for my life. Then again, I believe it is obvious Satan used these same four strategies to prevent the woman at the well from knowing God's great salvation. No doubt, he thought that because she had been married five times and was shacking-up with a man she was not married to, he was successful in advancing his agenda of thwarting God's plans and ravaging and destroying her life.

The woman at the well was delivered, as is made clear in the Scriptures. In fact, this social outcast turned soul-winner after taking that drink of Living Water. Now we are going to probe just a little deeper and find out what brought her to the point of being willing to talk to Jesus, listen to Him, and eventually trust Him as her Messiah.

~~~~~~~~~~~~~~~~~

After having her stomach pumped and receiving the 1,000 cc of coffee, Prisoner got up, went to the restroom, and then dressed and left the hospital for home. *Home—what is home?* Prisoner asked herself. *I'm not exactly sure what that is!* A million thoughts skipped back and forth through her mind. *People are bound to ask questions; how will I answer? If I ever have kids and they find out all of these things about their mother, will they still love me?* She was convinced that no one would love her if anything about her past was known to him or her, so she determined that if she ever had kids, everything within her power would be done to prevent their finding out about her past.

It was at least a month before Prisoner was able to go back to work, although she was not sure that she could face her coworkers when the time came. During that month at home, there was a lot of soul-searching, as she struggled to make sense of everything, which had happened. She was still uncertain why she had taken all those pills and whether or not she had really intended to do herself harm. Prisoner realized these questions would probably never be answered with absolute certainty, so she decided to dismiss them from her mind. One thing, however, that could not be dismissed from her mind, and for which she was grateful, was the unseen hand upon her shoulder. Had it not been for the touch of that unseen, special messenger, she would have surely died.

Prisoner finally was able to go back to work, but not without much difficulty. In a small town such as Sychar, people do not easily forget the wrong actions of another, and they were not willing to allow Prisoner to forget her wrongdoings either. There was always a lot of talking behind her back, and many glaring glances in her direction as she walked down the hall at work or down the street in town.

One day Prisoner went to work and found the other women in the factory all abuzz about the new male employee. He was especially nice to Prisoner and asked her for a date. She refused the first time he asked. However, the man was very persistent and continued to ask her for a date until she finally consented. She really enjoyed his company, so they spent a lot of time together.

Prisoner had vowed that she would never marry again, and she became a little nervous when he hinted he would like to spend the rest of his life with her. One day, he said he wanted to ask her something. She thought he was going to propose marriage and was concerned about how to say "no" without hurting him and without she being hurt also. It was not the man's intent to propose marriage at all; since he was prone to avoid long-term commitments, he, instead, asked her to move in with him.

"I don't know—I'll have to think about this," Prisoner replied.

"It's the perfect setup," the man pleadingly said. "—absolutely no strings attached. You and I can each come and go as we please, yet we will have companionship and not have to go through life alone."

Prisoner replied, "But I've always felt like that was sin."

"Do you really think you, of all people, should be analyzing what is sin and what is not sin?" the man intimidatingly asked. Intimidation was one thing Prisoner could not fight, so she reluctantly consented to live with this man.

Prisoner was still not happy, even though their relationship was just as the man had said it would be—there were no strings attached and each one could come and go as they pleased. Perhaps this *no-strings-attached* deal was not a good thing after all. Prisoner had failed again in her search for love, and she soon realized that there can be no love if there is no commitment. She felt guilty each time she went to bed with this man, but at least she had a place to live.

Before long, Prisoner was able to quit her job at the factory because the man she lived with provided very well for her. She was very thankful she could quit work, but this man's provisions for her made it practically impossible for her to ever move out. In other words, because of the depression and fatigue, she had grown very dependent upon him—dependent upon him to provide food, clothing, and shelter as well as love and emotional stability.

The days dragged on into weeks, weeks into months, and months into years. Although Prisoner had never grown accustomed to her pitiful state, she had come to accept it. *This is my destiny, my lot in life,* she thought. *I don't like it, but this is what fate has chosen for me. Why fight it? I might as well make the best of it—be thankful to have a roof over my head and food on the table. At least this man who shares his house, his money, and friendship with me has made the way whereby I don't have to go to work where everyone would force me to relive my past, day after day.* Every waking moment of every day, these thoughts played over and over in her mind as she tried to convince herself that her circumstances were evidence of who and what she was destined to be.

Some days, her depression and fatigue made it almost impossible for Prisoner to get out of bed. The man, whose house she shared, was a little outdone with all this, so Prisoner spent many nights alone while he was out on the town with other women. She finally decided to see a doctor in hopes that he would be able to help her depression. The doctor prescribed Prozac™ for Prisoner and told her she needed to stay on this medication for nine months to one year. After that time, he would gradually reduce the dosage and take her off the medicine.

It was only about a month before Prisoner was able to notice marked improvement in the way she felt and in her behavior. Although she still could not recall any good memories, at least she did not continually dwell on the bad memories. Overall, her health was better, she had more energy, and she was able to shed the few unwanted pounds, which she had gained over the past few years.

The best thing accomplished by taking the anti-depressant was the man she lived with wanted to spend more time with her. She did not dwell in the past, and the disconnectedness from self occurred less frequently, so in this respect, the medication was of great benefit to her. Sorry to say, however, she still felt as though she dwelt in another world from the people around her. Regrettably, authentic relationships were something Prisoner had heard about but had no clue as to what they entailed, and this sad circumstance was something not even Prozac™ could counteract.

The time came for Prisoner to begin the gradual reduction in the dosage of the antidepressant. Once the final dosage was taken, she did not notice any major changes in the way she felt or in her behavior. Sadly, though, in a few months after stopping the medication, she found nothing about her had changed—she was just as depressed and just as fatigued as she had always been. She tossed around the idea of going back to the doctor and requesting a renewal of the prescription for the antidepressant. This idea was soon dismissed as Prisoner reasoned there must be more to this life than looking forward to the next dose of medicine in order to feel halfway normal.

Prisoner awoke one morning to find the pumping system that supplied water to their house was not working. She told the man with whom she lived about the problem, but he said, "I can't check it now; I've got to get to work. Until I get home, you will have to get water from the well in the town square." Oh how she hated to go to that well! She hoped the problem was caused from something being wrong at their house only, so then she would not have to see the other townswomen gathered around the well. Much to her dismay, when she arrived at the well, all of the other women from town were there also. She heard one of the women say that, unfortunately, the problem lay with the central pumping system. The entire town of Sychar would need to draw water from the town well until new pumps could be shipped in and installed. No one knew exactly how long that would take.

Everyday, twice a day, Prisoner made the short trek from her house to the well and back again. She went to the well around six o'clock in the morning to draw enough water to make it through the day, then again at six o'clock in the evening to draw enough water to last through the night. Of course, all of the other townswomen went to draw water at the same times each day.

Prisoner saw their sneers. She heard their snide remarks. She saw their pointing accusing fingers in her direction. "Please, go and draw the water for me today!" she desperately pleaded.

The man replied with an emphatic, "No! Drawing water is woman's work. All of the other women draw the water for their households, so why can't you?"

"You know why I can't go to the well," Prisoner tearfully said. "I feel such shame; the other women treat me cruelly!"

"Well, that's too bad. I'm sorry they treat you mean. But I have to go to work; I don't have time to draw the water, so you'll just have to suck-it-up and make the best of things," the man said with a hint of aggravation in his voice.

Prisoner continued to go to the well every day for water. The beautiful way the golden morning sun glistened on the dew-kissed mountainside was never noticed by Prisoner. No matter what the sky was like or how bright the sun shone, the sky over Prisoner's head was always dark, always gloomy, almost as if she was walking through a dark gray tunnel with only an occasional pinpoint of light to be seen at the end of this *twilight zone* existence. She did not know how much longer she could continue to go on.

Thoughts and emotions swirled around and around in the muddy whirlpool of her mind, cyclically pulling them deeper until out of sight only to have them drift back to the surface again: *Will things ever change? Is there anyone who can rescue me or anyone willing to risk the attempt to rescue me? Will I ever be delivered from the prison, which holds me fast? I feel as though self is imprisoned by self. I must be delivered from self!*

As usual, Prisoner made her trek to the well around six o'clock on this particular evening, but as she would soon find out, there would be nothing usual about this occasion at the well. When she arrived at the well, the other women were there too of course, but in the midst of their gossiping and name-calling, she noticed a man sitting there at the well. As she approached the well, she noticed that the Man sitting there was a Jew.

The Man asked Prisoner for a drink. Although men did not normally converse with women in public, she was not surprised by the fact that a man would speak with her, especially considering the reputation she had acquired over the past few years. On the other hand, Prisoner was surprised that a Jew would ask a Samaritan for a drink. While Jews occasionally came through Samaria in order to engage in acts of commerce, for the most part Jews felt themselves to be far superior to the Samaritans and would not eat or drink from the same dishes that Samaritans used. Therefore, Prisoner said, "How come you, a Jew, are asking for a drink from me, a Samaritan? The Jews don't associate with the Samaritans?"

The Man was very kind and gentle; He simply replied, "If you knew the gift of God and who it is that is asking for a drink, you, instead, would have asked Him, and He would have given you Living Water."

Unable to fathom what He was saying, Prisoner said, "Sir, what are you talking about? The well is deep, you have nothing to draw the water with, and so from where did you get this Living Water?" Then she added, "Our ancestor, Jacob, gave us this well — he drank from it and watered his livestock from it, and they all died. Do you think that you are greater than he?"

The Man answered Prisoner in this way, "Everyone who drinks the water from this well will get thirsty again — it cannot satisfy. But, everyone who drinks the water that I will give him/her will never, ever thirst again! Furthermore, the water I give will be a well of water in them, springing up into everlasting life."

Prisoner, wanting to find a quick fix to her dilemma of having to suffer the maliciousness of the other townswomen, anxiously and desperately replied, "Give me this water so I won't be thirsty—so I'll never have to come back to this well and draw water!"

The Man responded to Prisoner's request in a manner that took her back for a few seconds. He told her, "Go call your husband and come back here."

Considering how she should answer this Man, Prisoner decided she would not need to lie. Simply telling Him she did not have a husband, should suffice, for this was the truth. This way, He would not know she was living with a man to whom she was not married. What He said next, really threw Prisoner for a loop! "I know that is true—you don't have a husband. For a fact, you've had five husbands, and the man you now have is not your husband."

How did He know? What must He think of me? Prisoner questioned within herself. *Perhaps I can change the subject,* she thought, *thus diverting His attention away from my many issues.* Prisoner said, "The more I observe you, I am beginning to see that you are a prophet." She then decided that if she brought up the subject of their differences concerning the proper place to worship that He would forget about her fornication. "Our ancestors worshiped here on Mt. Gerizim, but you Jews say that Jerusalem is the place to worship."

The Man continued to converse with Prisoner and show her the error of what she had always believed. "Woman, the time is coming when the Father will neither be worshiped on Mt. Gerizim nor in Jerusalem. As for you Samaritans, you worship that which you do not know, but, contrariwise, the Jews worship that which we know because salvation is from the Jews. However, a time is coming, in fact now is, when those who genuinely worship the Father will do so in spirit and in truth. You see, the Father is looking for authentic worshipers to worship Him. Because God is a Spirit, then He must be worshiped in the spiritual sphere and in the sphere of truth."

This Man definitely had Prisoner's attention, for she was intrigued at the words He spoke. Pondering what He had said about worship, she responded, "Some day, Messiah, the One called Christ, will come—I know this. When He comes, He will explain all these things and help us make sense of what we don't understand."

Then the Man looked Prisoner straight in the eye and told her, "I am He. I am the Messiah."

Prisoner was so excited that she abruptly discarded her water jar. It no longer mattered so much what others thought of her, for she left her water jar to never pick it up again. In discarding her water jar, which was filled with the garbage of a lifetime spent in the bondage of sin, at last she was able to break free from her past. She was changed—she was delivered from sin and from self! No longer will she be called *Prisoner*, but now she will be called *Freewoman—Delivered!*

She felt that she just had to tell someone, but whom could she tell about meeting the Messiah—who would listen to her? Delivered hurried to tell the only ones in town whom she thought would listen to her, the men. She knew the townswomen would not listen to her, but she very boldly told the men around town about the new Man in her life—the Messiah, the Christ!

~~~~~~~~~~~~~~~~~~~~~

HALLELUJAH! HALLELUJAH! At last, the woman at the well was delivered, and we can be free from the bondage of our pasts as well. The twenty-eighth verse of John chapter four, spoke to my heart as much or more than any verse in Scripture. We will never break the chains of our bondage as long as we remain determined to hold on to our water jars.

I know first handed that the water jar represents the many issues we refuse to deal with, and it is also indicative of our miserable attempts to satisfy our needs instead of trusting God to meet those needs. Refusing to deal with our past issues and continuing to stuff them into our water jars, is the reason that so many women, and men also, go from one rela-tionship, one marriage, to another and then another and then another. They spend a lifetime searching yet never finding what they are looking for, because they continue to look to another human being to satisfy a need only God can satisfy.

Right now, I am addressing the household of faith—those who have been born-again. Just because a person has been saved does not mean they have arrived at sinless perfection because we are still living in a fallen world and must deal with our fallen natures. God is moving in a great way among his children, but in the midst of God's working in our lives, there is still so much distress among His children. There is more depression, more addiction to drugs, alcohol, sex (heterosexual, bi-sexual, and same-sex), more fear, and more being married, divorced, and remarried numerous times than ever before.

I must stop and ask, "Dear Lord, why? Why have so many Christians bought into the lie that we must have, and that we deserve, instant gratification?" In general, we have convinced ourselves that: *If I do not feel the same thrill from my husband or wife I once did, it's okay to ditch them and find someone else. If my spouse does not make me feel loved, accepted, and affirmed, I will find someone who will—God understands—He wants me to be happy. God wants me to get rest and take care of my body, so if I can't sleep I'll take a pill to go to sleep and another to wake up and another pill when I'm anxious and another pill when I'm depressed...* This line of reasoning is the result of clinging to our water jars, instead of dealing with all of the issues within. Listen! This is idolatry. Any time we look to someone or something other than the Lord Jesus Christ to satisfy our needs and heal our wounded hearts, it is an act of idolatry; we have put a person, a relationship, and/or a medicine, etcetera, above God.

I remember my own bondage of days past. I have known hurt, feelings of worthlessness, shame, and injustices—but haven't we all? Oh sure, it had been years since I had allowed things before my eyes or into my ears that were displeasing to Holy God.

Gone were my days of throwing caution to the wind to engage in some ungodly, and potentially destructive, behavior. Nonetheless, I remained in bondage because I held tightly to my water jar in hopes that in its contents was something, whether it be doing good things or doing bad things, which would release me from the shame and guilt of my past.

There was not one shred of authenticity about me, and I withdrew from anyone who seemed to be halfway real. In fact, I had convinced myself my feelings of depression and disconnectedness were normal and that every *normal* person functioned this way. I had come to believe, not only were there consequences for wrongdoing, but that one must pay for the wrong action with enough good actions to make up the difference.

It was years, however, before I realized my continuing to carry my water jar was sin. Failing to understand my church work, my looking to my husband for affirmation, and, among many other things, my overeating in order to gain attention were acts of idolatry and pride, I was resolved to the false belief that this was my lot in life and nothing could be done to change it. Thus, my dysfunction continued because, although I did not realize it at the time, I was filled with foolish pride. Mrs. Gilbert states: "We are all dysfunctional to some degree because we have all 'fallen short of the glory of God' intended. … Most dysfunction remains because, 'it's all about me and my right to my pain.' We humans also have the tendency to not want to look at our own part in the dysfunction. …, but often the victim, rather than going to God, tries to take care of the pain by themselves." We must learn to let things go to God!

All of my life, I had looked to the contents of my water jar—being a good little girl, trying to please people, eating much more than I should, trying to buy friendship and love, and etcetera—in order that I might know the tiniest fragment of significance and self-worth. How slow of learning I am! Do not laugh—you are no different. I wanted to look in the mirror and say to myself, "Well duh! What took you so long to discover that those things never did work?"

Praise God for His marvelous grace, "grace that is greater than all my sin!" I wish I had learned sooner how to break the bondage of past sins, sins, which were forgiven but continued to enslave me. I finally came to the realization that I had left my water jar at Jesus' feet in exchange for salvation, but the first time I was hurt, felt shame, was afraid, felt unloved, and etcetera, I went back and picked up my water jar instead of trusting Jesus to meet every need in my heart. I continued in this vicious cycle of laying down my water jar—picking it up again—laying it down again—picking it up again, until it became so burdensome I threw up my hands and said, "What's the use!" Nevertheless, at just the right time, God's Holy Spirit illumined for me verse twenty-eight of John chapter four. "She left her water jar"—these five little words transformed my thinking and delivered me from myself.

Suddenly, on this particular day, I realized that nowhere in Scripture is it ever recorded the woman at the well went back and picked up the water jar she had left at the feet of Jesus. I love the way Kenneth S. Wuest, in 1961, translated this verse in *The New Testament: An Expanded Translation*: "Thereupon, the woman **abruptly discarded** her water jar" (John 4:28a; emphasis mine). Each time I read this particular translation, I get a mental picture of the woman at the well dropping, almost throwing down, her water jar as though it were a hot potato about to burn her hands. I wanted to know the freedom in Christ I had heard others speak of having! At last, I would break out of my prison cell because I finally understood that I must follow this woman's example—get rid of the water jar.

Therefore, I abruptly discarded my water jar. I determined I must deal with my issues rather than stuffing them away or masking them with some means of medication in order to give the impression I was happy, whether or not the medication used was drugs, good works, or overeating or eating too little.

Please, allow me to make a statement here for the sake of clarity. It is not my intention to hurt or discredit anyone with this book. Quite the contrary—I desire that you become free, and I know, first-handedly, you will never know true freedom unless you are willing to deal with all issues of the past and learn to handle circumstances that arise in healthy ways, which are in agreement with God's word.

Good works with the wrong motives, overeating, and refusal to eat what is needed to be healthy are all sins—this fact is a no-brainer. On the other hand, doctor prescribed drugs may sometimes be necessary, but should be taken along with Godly, Bible-based counseling. Mrs. Gilbert gives this insight: "I do believe that antidepressants are over-prescribed, much like the gastric bypass surgery has now become the quick-fix for obesity. But I also know we have to be careful not to stigmatize those brothers and sisters who truly need medication. In the past, it has been difficult for anyone in the Christian community to talk about their mental health problems without feeling like a failure." Therefore, I am not saying it is wrong to take medication for depression and/or anxiety, nor am I indicating that a Christian who needs medication is a failure. I am merely stressing that medication should never be used as the total solution to our problems because, in doing so, we sometimes miss God's teaching and direction for our lives.

To further clarify, I offer this quote by Mike Benoit, a Christian psychologist: "There are many good reasons to be wary about beginning antidepressants, beyond the side-effects, which are fewer and more manageable in the second generation drugs, there is some evidence that permanent changes may occur in the structure of the brain over long-term use. For instance, if one changes how much of a neurotransmitter is available in the brain, then the brain areas that produce that neurotransmitter may slow down production. Additionally, using medication to lift mood when the factors that have caused depression are not addressed, just postpones the problem. Pain is motivational. A moderate level of psychological pain can drive a person to change things about his or her life. If the pain is relieved by medication, there may be less motivation to act. ..."

I never cease to be amazed at God's love for me. Even now, when I look back on all my pain, God's fingerprints are so explicitly seen on my life. I now understand the true meaning of the adage, "No pain; no gain." It was because of God's love for me, individually, that He allowed everything that came my way. I am truly grateful to my Heavenly Father that my pain was not relieved, and therefore I was motivated to *act*, seek His face. If it had not been for the pain, I would have never learned to leave my water jar, and I would still be enslaved—perhaps wearing a smile most of the time, but a prisoner nonetheless.

While "I press toward the mark for the prize of the high calling of God in Christ Jesus" (Philippians 3:14, KJV), I do not dwell *on* my past nor *in* my past. Yet, on the other hand, I will not forget what it was like to be in such bondage, in order that I may never take for granted the freedom of His grace or the wonderful feeling of having been delivered.

Freedom! What a word! *Freedom*! What a feeling! *Freedom*! What a beautiful, wonderful, sweet, glorious, indescribable state! Freedom—what your Heavenly Father desires for you!

CHAPTER SEVEN

Directive for Freedom

I t is my intent for this final chapter to present some very practical instruction in becoming free and remaining free. My desire for each of you is that you know and walk in freedom—that you are strengthened to the point where you can leave your water jar, once for all. Therefore, I do not intend to beat around the bush—I will be very frank and to the point.

The first step of knowing freedom is, of course, to be saved. There must be a point in time when you know, beyond a shadow of a doubt, you left your water jar at Jesus' feet and received that drink of Living Water. If you have never trusted Christ as your Savior, I invite you to do so now. Simply admit you are a sinner (Romans 3:23) in need of a Savior, that your sin deserves punishment, but that Jesus took your punishment and offered you eternal life (Romans 6:23), believe in your heart that Christ died,

157

was buried, and raised from the dead (Romans 10:9-10), and call on Him to save you (Romans 10:13).

If the matter of your salvation has been settled, then you need to grow in your faith. "Like newborn infants, desire the unadulterated spiritual milk, so that you may grow by it in your salvation, since you have tasted that the Lord is good" (1Peter 2:2-3, HCSB). If you will recall from chapter two, if we do not grow in our faith, we will become desensitized to the Holy Spirit's teaching and guiding us. Thus, failure to grow up in Christ results in our going back to the well for our water jar. The first measure we must take in growing in our walk with Christ is to know the truth. "And ye shall know the truth, and the truth shall make you free" (John 8:32, KJV). Knowing the truth is what makes us free, so how can we know truth? John chapter seventeen verse seventeen tells us, "… thy word is truth." It becomes quite clear, then, that in order to know truth we must know God's word. I will let you in on a little secret; John chapter eight verse thirty-one comes directly before John chapter eight verse thirty-two. Verse thirty-one states, "… If ye continue in my word, *then* are ye my disciples indeed;" (John 8:31, KJV). It is impossible to be a learner of Jesus Christ apart from knowing the Bible, for the Bible, the written word, is Jesus, the Living Word, written on paper.

Do whatever is necessary to know God's word. It is best to open the Scriptures first thing every morning, but if that is not possible, find some time during the day to hear what your Heavenly Father is saying to you in His word. Only for five minutes every day, is better than many days with no time in the word. FIVE MINUTES—surely your freedom is worth that much.

We will not run for our water jar every time we face a crisis if we will pray constantly and confess our sins. "Pray without ceasing" (1Thessalonians 5:17, NKJV). This verse needs no further explanation; however, I would like to remind you that to "pray without ceasing" is a command, not a suggestion. If Christians would obey this command, then when we are put to the test, prayer will be our first choice, not our last chance. Nothing destroys the fellowship God desires to have with us like sins, which we have not been willing to confess. Therefore, when we sin, whether in word or in deed, we should immediately confess it as sin and repent. "If we confess our sins, he is faithful and just to forgive us *our* sins, and to cleanse us from all unrighteousness" (1John 1:9, KJV).

Is the Lord worthy of our praise? What a question! Of course He is worthy of our praise! Then why are Christians, His children, recipients of His mercy and grace, so reluctant to praise Him? Just as First Thessalonians chapter five verse seventeen is a command, so First Thessalonians chapter five verse sixteen is also a command, "Rejoice always" (NKJV). Let us not forget the many times the Psalmists gave praise to the one and only true God and told us to do likewise: "Let everything that has breath praise the LORD. Praise the LORD!" (Psalm 150:5, NKJV). God is worthy of our praise, and God deserves all honor and praise. However, God commands us to praise Him **for our good**, not His. When **we praise** the Lord, He spiritually **nourishes us** through that praise (Nehemiah 8:10).

If you have been enslaved by your water jar, then in order to be free, you must change your thinking. Because you have believed the enemy's lies for so long, a faulty belief system concerning whom and what you are, and concerning your perspective of right and wrong, has been firmly set in place and must be broken down and replaced with truth. You will never be able to permanently leave your water jar until you decide to change your thinking and begin to think as Christ thinks.

Wrong thinking always results, sooner or later, in wrong behavior, even when the behavior appears to be something good. In other words, the behavior or action in and of itself may be good, such as the work you are involved in at church, but if your motives for doing these *good things* are impure, then the behavior is wrong and is the result of wrong thinking. The only solution is to change the way we think so it lines up with truth, the Bible.

We are urged, "… to present your bodies as a living sacrifice, holy and pleasing to God; this is your spiritual worship. Do not be conformed to this age, but be transformed by the renewing of your mind, so that you may discern what is the good, pleasing, and perfect will of God" (Romans 12:1b-2, HCSB). A passive approach to changing the way you think will not yield lasting results. Instead, you must choose to be aggressive in the abolishment of the lies and false beliefs through being transformed by the renewing of your mind.

The world is vying for control of our minds—the way we think. We are bombarded from all sides as the world attempts to squeeze us into their mould of having a secular worldview, as opposed to a Biblical worldview. The combatant to this world's ploy of forcing us to think as they think is to be transformed by the renewing of our minds. Our thinking must be changed by undergoing a renovation, a remodeling, of our thought-life. You can be assured, the remodeling job the Holy Spirit does on our minds far surpasses anything you will see on *Extreme Makeover, Home Edition©®™*. The philosophies of this world will take us captive (Colossians 2:8) if we do not make the conscious choice to prevent this from happening.

Where do your affections lie? The Apostle Paul instructs us, "Set your affection on things above, not on things on the earth" (Colossians 3:2, KJV). When we are earthly minded, when we are caught up with living, when our affection is fixed on things of this world, we are bogged down by the cares of this life, and in the realization of how needy we have become, we look to things or people to satisfy our need rather than trusting God. It is this mindset, the mindset of the flesh, that enslaves us because the mindset of the flesh is death, but the mindset of the Spirit is life and peace (Romans 8:6).

It is of utmost importance we not only choose to change our thinking, but we must also be diligent to replace wrong thinking with right thinking. You may be wondering exactly what that means or how to accomplish this. A great place to begin this renovation of your mind is to follow the teaching of Philippians chapter four verse eight. "Finally brethren, whatever things are true, whatever things are noble, whatever things are just, whatever things are pure, whatever things are lovely whatever things are of good report, if there is any virtue and if there is anything praise-worthy—meditate on these things" (NKJV).

In order to leave the water jar and never look to its contents for love, approval, acceptance, and significance, we need to understand the love God has for each of us, individually. I had the outlandish misconception that God loved me enough to give His only Son to pay the penalty for my sin, but in order to gain His approval and acceptance, I must perform well enough—jump through enough hoops—then He would not only love me, but also like me.

A young man I know said that his grandmother attributes the cause of every sin to pride. Whenever something is said about a particular sin she replies, "It's that pride thing." I am beginning to believe this grandmother is correct in her evaluation concerning the root of every sin. Although I did not realize it at the time, it was the sin of pride that caused me to think I could be good enough, perform well enough, and/or engage in enough activity to gain God's acceptance.

Paul, in chapter one of his letter to the Ephesians— if we will open our spiritual ears and hear—tells us that we are blessed with **every** spiritual blessing in the heavenly places in Christ. He then goes on to explain what this spiritual blessing contains: We are chosen; we are adopted; He made us accepted;

we have redemption; we have forgiveness; we have obtained an inheritance, and we are sealed with the Holy Spirit. God's acceptance of us is not based on what we do or what we do not do, but we are accepted because of what Christ did on Calvary's cross. Allow this truth to settle into your heart! This is the position that we as born-again believers have in Christ.

God thinks only good thoughts for us (Jeremiah 29:11), and even when He tests us and puts us through the refining fire, it is because of His love for us (Psalm 66:10-12). Our Heavenly Father does not withhold any good thing from His children; on the contrary, at the moment we were saved, we received everything God is, everything God does, and every-thing God provides (2Peter 1:2-3). His love is uncon-ditional and unfailing. So great is God's love for us that nothing can separate us from His love—not even we, ourselves (Romans 8:35-39).

Furthermore, God has promised to "supply all your need according to His riches in glory by Christ Jesus" (Philippians 4:19, NKJV). If God will supply every need, then why do we search in other places to have our needs met? We must emphatically seek Him above all else and ardently resolve that Jesus is more than enough! It is time to declare, "My value as a person is not found in things or activity, but in my relationship with God as my Father!"

Finally, it is not enough to understand our position in Christ and the love the Father has for us; we also need to verbalize these truths. The reason we need to speak these truths is verbalization of the truth aids in the internalization of that truth into our minds. By speaking the truth, I do not mean we have the ability to create reality by speaking or not speaking. For example, some people today erroneously teach that we will either be physically sick or well depending on the words we speak, the things we confess.

However, it is important to note that everyone talks to himself or herself, either audibly or silently. Thus the question is, "What are you telling yourself?" Whatever we have come to believe about ourselves, whether it is truth or lies, is what we speak to ourselves, for the Scripture says, "I believed, therefore I spoke" (2Corinthians 4:13b, HCSB). The things that you tell yourself will eventually be manifested in your behavior, right behavior for truth and wrong behavior for lies, accordingly.

Eventually, what you have come to believe about yourself you will speak, and the words you hear from your mouth serve to reinforce the belief. The belief, in turn, reinforces the words, and the belief and the words together play out in our actions. Each of these, the belief, the words, and the actions feeds one off the others. One reason that many Christians have such difficulty allowing the light of Christ to shine through them is because their self-talk is contrary to the truth of God's word. For example, if I constantly tell myself that I am worthless and/or trash, I will continue to believe these things about myself, and I will begin to live in a manner that says to everyone else I am worthless and/or trash. Likewise, if I constantly tell myself that I am superior to other people, I will continue to believe that I am superior, I will be lifted up with pride, and begin to live in a manner that says to everyone else that I am arrogant and snobbish.

As I began to deal with the many issues in my water jar, I was astounded to realize just how many lies I had believed throughout my lifetime. I had believed the lie that in order for people to love me, it was necessary for me to prove to them that I was deserving of their love and acceptance. In the same way, I believed the lie that there was nothing, not one single thing, good about my growing up years and much of my adult years.

Over the years, I had done some hefty trash talking to myself, all under the guise of humility. I immediately went face-to-the-floor when I realized I had grieved the Holy Spirit and deeply hurt my God, my Creator, who formed me in my mother's womb and put me on this planet to fulfill His purpose for my life. My self-talk had been completely contrary to what my Heavenly Father says to me and about me, and this was sin. Therefore, I confessed the lies and my false beliefs as sin, repented, and began speaking truth to myself. After repenting of my sin, God allowed me to regain some good memories from my childhood and early adulthood. I cannot thank Him enough!

You, my sisters and brothers, need to speak the truth. Get into the word, read God's promises, and read what He has to say about you. Read aloud your identity as a believer that is found in Ephesians chapter one. Our Enemy cannot read our minds, but he does hear our words. No doubt, he has heard you speaking lies to yourself and about yourself often enough, so it is time for him to hear you speak the truth. He cannot bear to hear the truth of God's word, so open your Bible, read it aloud, and shove it in the devil's face.

Do not entertain a lie for even one second—speak the truth. In addition, it is good, from time to time, to tell Satan to leave you alone. "DEVIL, GET OUT OF MY FACE! I KNOW WHO YOU ARE AND WHAT YOU ARE! BETTER YET, I KNOW WHO I AM AND WHAT I AM—I AM A CHILD OF THE KING, AN HEIR WITH GOD AND A JOINT HEIR WITH JESUS! JESUS IS MY SAVIOR, MY BIG BROTHER, MY PROTECTOR, MY PROVIDER, MY DELIVERER! I AM VALUABLE TO GOD! I AM VICTORIOUS BECAUSE OF CHRIST! I AM FREE!"

You, dear friend, have been a prisoner far too long, haunted by your past failures. Now is the time for you to break free from the bondage of past sins, and now is the time to break the chains of passing those destructive behaviors to your children and your children's children. Deal with the issues of the past, then leave your water jar at the feet of Jesus, and never pick it up again. If the woman at the well can do this, so can you. Jesus is more than enough to satisfy every need and to heal every hurt. Can you see Him? He is standing at the well with open arms, waiting for you to bring your water jar and leave it with Him so He can show you the wonderful plans He has for you, and so you can finally know the freedom that comes from trusting Him, completely.

Lightning Source UK Ltd.
Milton Keynes UK
UKHW011455060720
366107UK00004B/1114

9 781604 778526